Syria

Syria

BY PATRICIA K. KUMMER

Enchantment of the World
Second Series

Children's Press®
A Division of Scholastic Inc.

NEW YORK TORONTO LONDON AUCKLAND SYDNEY
MEXICO CITY NEW DELHI HONG KONG
DANBURY, CONNECTICUT

Frontispiece: Ancient ruins at Palmyra

Consultant: Dr. Paul Sprachman, Rutgers University, Center for Middle Eastern Studies

Please note: All statistics are as up-to-date as possible at the time of publication.

Book production by Herman Adler Design

Library of Congress Cataloging-in-Publication Data

Kummer, Patricia K.
    Syria / by Patricia K. Kummer.
        p. cm. — (Enchantment of the world. Second series)
    Includes bibliographical references and index.
    ISBN 0-516-23677-6
    1. Syria—Juvenile literature. I. Title. II. Series.
    DS93.K86 2005
    956.91—dc22   2005005706

CHILDREN'S PRESS and associated logos are trademarks and/or registered
trademarks of Scholastic Library Publishing. SCHOLASTIC and associated logos
are trademarks and/or registered trademarks of Scholastic Inc.
1 2 3 4 5 6 7 8 9 10 R 14 13 12 11 10 09 08 07 06 05

Acknowledgments

The author would like to thank the staff of the Lisle Library District for their help in locating sources on Syria that were as up-to-date as possible.

Contents

Cover photo:
A Druze man
from Syria

Grazing sheep

A devout Muslim
reading the Quran

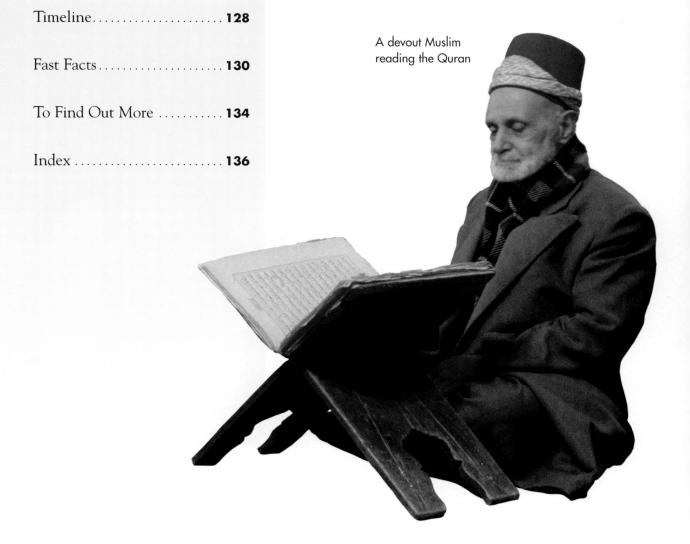

CHAPTER
ONE

Past and Present

SANDY BROWN PILLARS RISE IN THE RUINED CITY OF PALMYRA in the Syrian Desert. Huge wooden waterwheels groan as they lift water from the Orontes River. Christian pilgrims follow the steps of Saint Paul down Straight Street in Damascus. The domes and minarets of ancient mosques—Muslim houses of worship—dominate city skylines. In Syria, the past is always present.

Syria, however, is not merely a country filled with ancient ruins and religious sites. Oil derricks also rise above the desert.

Opposite: **Ruins of Palmyra**

The Al-Rahman Mosque towers above Aleppo.

Past and Present **9**

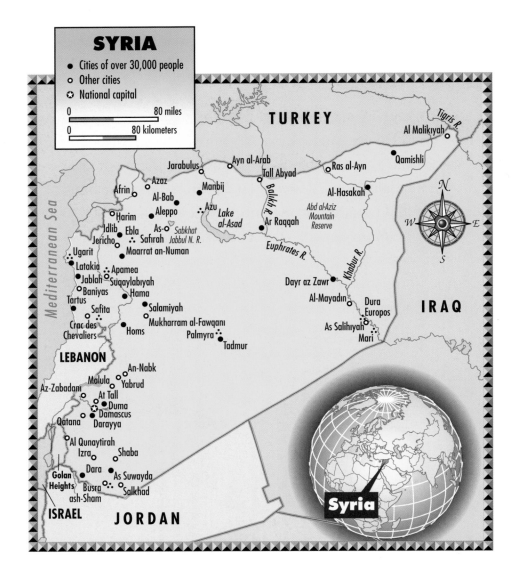

SYRIA

- ● Cities of over 30,000 people
- ○ Other cities
- ✪ National capital

0   80 miles

0   80 kilometers

TURKEY

IRAQ

LEBANON

ISRAEL

JORDAN

Mediterranean Sea

Tigris R.

Al Malikıyah

Qamishli

Ayn al-Arab

Ras al-Ayn

Jarabulus

Tall Abyad

Al-Hasakah

Azaz

Manbij

Afrin

Al-Bab

Azu

Lake al-Asad

Harim

Aleppo

Ar Raqqah

Abd al-Aziz Mountain Reserve

Idlib

Ebla

As-

Sabkhat Jabbul N. R.

Jericho

Safirah

Ugarit

Maarrat an-Numan

Euphrates R.

Khabur R.

Balikh R.

Latakia

Apamea

Jablah

Suqaylabıyah

Dayr az Zawr

Baniyas

Hama

Tartus

Al-Mayadın

Dura Europos

Safita

Salamiyah

As Salihıyah

Crac des Chevaliers

Mukharram al-Fawqanı

Mari

Homs

Palmyra

Tadmur

An-Nabk

Malula

Yabrud

Az-Zabadanı

At Tall

Duma

Damascus

Qatana

Darayya

Al Qunaytirah

Izra

Shaba

Golan Heights

Dara

As Suwayda

Busra ash-Sham

Salkhad

Syria

Dams control the flow of the Euphrates and Orontes rivers. Universities, sports stadiums, office buildings, huge hotels, and airports are part of city life. Television antennae and satellite dishes stick up from apartment buildings. Syria has a long history, but it is a modern country that is changing quickly.

Syrians take pride in their land's rich history. In fact, the country's current slogan is "Syria Today: 5,000 Years in the Making." Syria's history is the story of thousands of years of migration and invasion. Syria's geography made it easy for people to enter the land.

Early "Sea People" and later Crusaders came across the Mediterranean Sea and landed on Syria's beaches. Gaps in the low-lying mountains gave them access to Syria's interior. Wide-open plains, steppes, and deserts allowed entry to other groups. Canaanites, Aramaeans, and Arabs entered from the south. Assyrians, Babylonians, and Persians came from the east. Hittites and Ottoman Turks invaded from the north.

The Assyrians built magnificent palaces, such as the Palaces at Nimrud (above), in what is now Iraq.

Arabic is the dominant language in Syria.

Most Syrians today are a blend of the many peoples who settled or invaded the land. The Muslim Arabs had the longest-lasting effect. Today, 90 percent of Syrians are Muslim, and Syria's official language is Arabic.

Problems of a Young Country

Although Syria's history is more than 5,000 years old, Syria didn't become an independent country until 1946. Before that time, Syrians had little experience in governing themselves. Because of this, Syria went through twenty-five years of political instability. The unstable governments did little to develop the young country's economy.

In 1970, Hafiz al-Asad gained power. He served as Syria's president from 1971 until his death in 2000. During those years, al-Asad held tight control over Syria's government and economy. He made some progress in Syria's economic development, but the Syrian people had few political rights.

Since 2000, Hafiz's son Bashar al-Asad has been Syria's president. Under the younger al-Asad, Syria's government has loosened some of the restrictions on speech, press, and assembly. Bashar has allowed more privately owned businesses to open as well. Syria is also beginning to take a larger role in the world. Asad has negotiated several trade treaties with European nations. But Syria remains a socialist republic with one-man rule by the president. Because all changes must be approved by the president, change will continue to come slowly for the nation and for the Syrian people.

For now, Syrians continue life as usual. In the cities of Damascus, Aleppo, Homs, Latakia, and Hama, they socialize with friends and family in their homes. They eat and talk at cafés. They pray at mosques. Syrians are renowned for their warmth and hospitality. It is these everyday interactions with friends and family that are at the center of their lives.

Bashar al-Asad took over as president of Syria after his father died.

The Heart of the Middle East

14

SYRIA IS IN THE HEART OF THE MIDDLE EAST, THE PART of the world where Europe, Asia, and Africa meet. Turkey lies to the north of Syria; Iraq to the east and south; Jordan to the south; and Israel, Lebanon, and the Mediterranean Sea to the west. Europeans call Syria and other countries on the eastern end of the Mediterranean Sea "the Levant." This means "rising" in French. It refers to the fact that for people of the Mediterranean, the sun rises over Syria. In Arabic, Syria is referred to as *sha'm*, or "the northern area." This is because the name came from people living in Saudi Arabia, to the south.

Syria covers 71,504 square miles (185,170 square kilometers), making it about the same size as North Dakota in the United States. This area includes the Golan Heights, a part of Syria currently occupied by Israel.

Opposite: **A water vendor at work in Damascus**

Syrians climb a hillside in the Golan Heights.

Land Along the Coast

Syria's coastline extends about 120 miles (190 km) along the Mediterranean Sea between Lebanon and Turkey. In the north, the coast is marked by rocky inlets and cliffs. But south of that rough coastline, white, sandy beaches stretch for miles. Syria's coast is wet and warm. The region receives about 35 inches (89 centimeters) of rain each year. Temperatures range from a winter average of 50° Fahrenheit (10° Celsius) to a summer average of 84°F (29°C).

Some of Syria's most fertile land lies near the coast. With good soil and a favorable climate, farmers in this area can grow crops throughout the year. Most of the country's vegetables and fruits come from the coastal plain. Apple, cherry, peach, and apricot trees grow in orchards. Groves of orange and lemon trees also flourish.

Orchards blanket parts of Syria.

Syria's Geographic Features

Area: 71,504 square miles (185,170 sq km)

Greatest Distance East to West: 515 miles (829 km)

Greatest Distance North to South: 465 miles (748 km)

Longest Shared Border: 510 miles (822 km) with Turkey

Coastline: 120 miles (193 km) along the Mediterranean Sea

Highest Elevation: Mount Hermon in Israeli-occupied Golan Heights, 9,232 feet (2,814 m) above sea level

Lowest Elevation: Near Lake Tiberias, 656 feet (200 m) below sea level

Longest River: Euphrates, 415 miles (670 km) through Syria

Largest Lake: Mamlahat al-Jabbul, 60 square miles (155 sq km), southeast of Aleppo

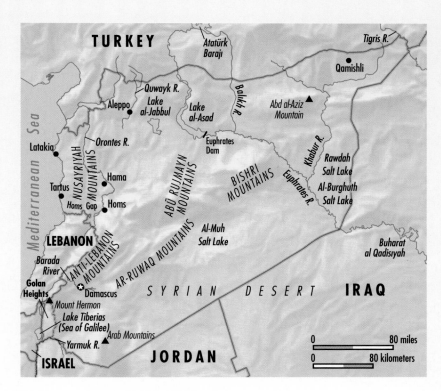

Mountain Ranges

The Nusayriyah Mountains are directly east of Syria's coast. They extend north to south from Turkey to Lebanon. For the most part, the Nusayriyah Mountains form a barrier between the coast and Syria's interior. In the south, however, there is a break in the mountains called the Homs Gap. This gap allows easy access from the coast to Syria's interior. Syria's oil pipeline runs through the Homs Gap to the port city of Tartus.

Sheep graze on Syria's scrubby grasslands.

The western side of the Nusayriyah Mountains catch the rain from the Mediterranean Sea. This area receives about 45 inches (114 cm) of rain each year. Snow falls on the mountaintops. Syria's largest stands of forest are on the western side of the Nusayriyah Mountains. Olive trees, lime trees, and tobacco grow in terraces that farmers have built on the western mountainsides. But little rain reaches the eastern side of these mountains. The scrub grasses that grow there are good for grazing sheep and goats.

Farther to the south, the Anti-Lebanon Mountains mark Syria's border with Lebanon. In the southern part of these mountains, Mount Hermon rises to 9,232 feet (2,814 meters). It is Syria's highest point. Mount Hermon is in a region called the Golan Heights. In 1967, Israel captured the Golan Heights during the Six-Day War. The area remains occupied by Israel. Syria's lowest point is also in the Golan Heights. Lake Tiberias, which is also called the Sea of Galilee, is 656 feet (200 m) below sea level.

Several other mountain ranges lie in Syria. The Arab Mountains in southwestern Syria are extinct volcanoes. The eastern side of these mountains are marked by lava flows and caves. The Abu Rujmayn and the Bishri mountains rise in Syria's desert. Northeastern Syria has Abd al-Aziz Mountain.

Mount Hermon is Syria's highest peak.

A vast plain lies east of the Nusayriyah and Anti-Lebanon Mountains. This plain forms an arc that stretches from Jordan north to Turkey. The arc then turns east along the border with Turkey. The plain, which contains some of Syria's richest soil, is also known as Syria's steppe. A steppe is a treeless plain with enough rainfall to grow large crops of grain. Syria's steppe receives up to 20 inches (51 cm) of rain each year. Average temperatures on the steppe can reach 99°F (37°C) in the summer. Temperatures fall to an average 34°F (4°C) in the winter.

Many rivers flow through or along Syria's steppe. These include the Yarmuk, Barada, Orontes, Quwayk, Euphrates, and Khabur. The waters from these rivers help Syria's farmers. In

The Euphrates River flows through eastern Syria.

some places, floodwaters enrich the soil of nearby land. In other places, irrigation systems link the rivers to the steppe's fields. Syria's largest inland cities and towns developed along these rivers. They include Damascus, Homs, Hama, Aleppo, and Qamishli.

Damascus, Syria's capital, spreads out across the southern steppe.

The Syrian steppe contains several subregions. The Hauran covers most of the southern tip of Syria. Black basalt rock formed by lava marks much of the Hauran. Large wheat and barley crops grow in the Hauran's rich volcanic soil. North of the Hauran is the lush, green Ghouta. This is an oasis of about 120 square miles (310 sq km) that surrounds Damascus. The Ghouta, which is watered by the Barada River, is a fertile region where many fruits and vegetables are grown.

Women use pitchforks to harvest wheat.

The subregion of the Ghab lies northwest of Hama. This was once a great swamp on the Orontes River. Between 1954 and 1968, the swamp was drained and dams were built on the river. From the dam, water moves through irrigation canals to fields. Wheat and barley now grow in the Ghab in winter. Cotton, rice, and sugar beets grow in summer. Farther north, the Central Plains surround the city of Aleppo. The plains receive enough rain each year to support large crops of cotton, sugar beets, and wheat.

In far northeastern Syria lies the Jazira, Syria's largest area of fertile land. *Jazira* means "island," and this region is like an island between the Euphrates and Tigris rivers. Wheat and cotton are the Jazira's main crops. Most of Syria's oil and natural gas deposits lie below the ground in the Jazira.

The Syrian Desert

The Syrian Desert covers more than half of Syria. The Euphrates River marks the eastern limits of this huge desert, while Syria's steppe borders the desert to the north and west. To the south and southeast, the desert spills into Jordan and Iraq. The western part of the desert is hard, rocky land. Desert sands begin farther east. The Syrian Desert has hot, dry summers and cold winters. At most, it receives about 5 inches (13 cm) of rain per year. When the rains come, streambeds called *wadis* fill and overflow. The heat of the desert soon dries up the

Bedouins drill for water in the Syrian Desert.

wadis. Temperatures can reach as high as 114°F (45°C) in the summer.

There are a few green spots in the middle of the Syrian Desert. In these oases, short grasses and a few trees grow. The Bedouin, nomadic desert people, graze their sheep, camels, and horses at these oases. Syria's largest oasis is at Tadmur. The Romans called this place Palmyra, meaning "city of palms." Today, the area around Tadmur has one of Syria's few forested areas.

Looking at Syria's Cities

Aleppo is either Syria's largest or second-largest city. Because careful population counts are not done in Syria, it is unclear whether Aleppo or the capital city of Damascus is larger. Aleppo is located in northwestern Syria on the Quwayk River. One of the world's oldest cities, it was founded about 3000 B.C. Aleppo has been a center of trade since ancient times. Today, it is a major textile center. It is home to a large Christian minority, made up mostly of Armenians. Aleppo's largest landmark is the ruins of the Citadel (below), a fortress that stands upon a high rock outcropping. Other important historical buildings include the Grand Mosque, the *souq* (an enclosed marketplace), and ancient bathhouses that are still used today.

Outside of Aleppo stand Syria's ghost towns, known as the Dead Cities. Christians abandoned these 600 villages when Arab Muslims invaded Syria in A.D. 635. The churches and other buildings were made from large blocks of rock. Many of them are still standing today.

Homs is Syria's third-largest city. It lies about halfway between Aleppo and Damascus on the Orontes River. It also has easy access to the Mediterranean Sea, which makes it one of Syria's trading centers. Homs's main industries are the refining of oil and sugar. The city was founded more than 2,200 years ago. Ruins of the old city walls can still be seen.

Latakia is Syria's fourth-largest city. Located on the Mediterranean Sea, it is the country's largest port. Latakia was founded in about 1000 B.C. and named in about 290 B.C. by one of Alexander the Great's generals. Today, Latakia is a busy city, known for its sandy beach and its souq.

Syria's fifth-largest city is Hama. It is located on the Orontes River about 50 miles (80 km) north of Homs. Hama's history can be traced back to at least 1000 B.C. Much of the city was destroyed in 1982 when government troops squashed a rebellion there. Still standing, however, are seventeen *norias*, huge wooden waterwheels that are part of the area's irrigation system. The Azem Palace and the Grand Mosque (above) are other points of interest in Hama.

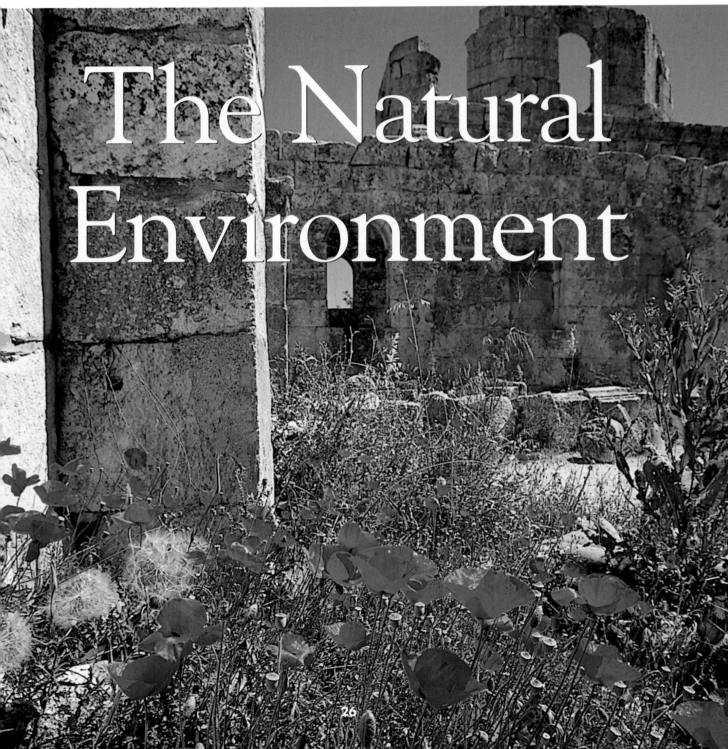

The Natural Environment

Trees flourish alongside rivers and streams.

DESERT COVERS MORE THAN HALF OF SYRIA. IN THIS LAND of shifting sands, it is so hot and so dry that most plants and animals cannot eke out an existence. Syria's mountains and steppe are more welcoming to living things. But even there, plants and animals sometimes struggle to survive.

Plant Life

Forests are rare in Syria. They cover only about 3 percent of the land. Pine trees, fir trees, and cedars grow in the north on the rainy, western side of the Nusayriyah Mountains. Oaks and other hardwood trees grow on the southern end of the Nusayriyah Mountains. Plants that do not need much water grow on the eastern side of the mountains. These include boxwood, myrtle, and wild olives. Scrubby underbrush plants such as garigue and maquis also grow on the mountains. A few

Opposite: **Flowers bloom at the Saint Simeon ruins near Aleppo.**

The Damascus Rose

The most popular flower in Syria is the Damascus rose. The flower's bright blooms have an unusually strong scent. Syrians consider the rose a symbol of originality and beauty. Every year in the spring, Damascus hosts an international flower show. The Damascus rose always has a prominent place at the fair. Products made from the roses, such as rose water, honey, and seasonings, are also honored.

cedar, cypress, oak, and pine trees survive in the Anti-Lebanon Mountains. Hawthorn and terebinth trees are found in the steppe. Date palms grow in the Euphrates Valley.

In the early spring, blue, pink, and yellow wildflowers decorate the land. By summer, the searing heat causes them to wilt and die. Their seeds drop onto the ground and await the rain that will help them bloom again. Several types of irises also bloom in Syria.

Animal Life

Syria has about 130 kinds of mammals. The bear is Syria's largest animal. Other mammals include deer, foxes, hyenas, jackals, and wild pigs. The gray wolf is a threatened species in Syria. Many herders hunt the wolves to protect their livestock. A few golden hamsters still live in Syria. Most of the golden hamsters that are sold as pets around the world are descendants of a pregnant hamster that was caught in Syria in the 1930s.

The Syrian brown bear is smaller than its cousin, the North American grizzly bear.

Syria's desert animals include graceful gazelles and jerboas, which are rodents that jump. Chameleons, lizards, and a variety of snakes live in Syria's desert. An important desert animal is the camel. At one time, camels were the main form of transportation for the Bedouin, a nomadic people who live in the Syrian Desert. Now, many Bedouins use trucks, but about thirteen thousand camels still live in Syria. Bedouins ride them in camel races, and tourists ride them for a sense of adventure.

Bedouins prepare for a camel race.

Arabian Horses

Although Syria does not have a national animal, the country is proud of its Arabian horses. These strong, elegant horses were traditionally bred by Bedouins. The horses are so well adapted to the desert that the Bedouins consider them a gift from Allah. The Syrian government regards them as a special treasure and records information about each horse in the *Syrian Arab Horse Stud Book*. Only purebred Arabians make it into this book.

A pelican feeds by putting its head underwater and scooping up fish with its large beak.

Syria has about 360 different kinds of birds. Flamingoes, pelicans, ducks, and geese nest near water. Geese and ducks are also found in the steppe, where they feed on grain in the fields. Buzzards, eagles, and peregrine falcons make nests in mountain cliffs. The saker falcon lives in mountains, the steppe, and the desert. In Syria, it is an endangered species.

About 1,500 different kinds of insects fly or crawl around Syria. Mosquitoes are common in moist areas. Sand flies abound in the desert. And grasshoppers live in the steppe. Sometimes locusts swarm into fields of grain and devour an entire crop within a few minutes.

Pigeons in Damascus

Pigeons are common birds in cities throughout the world. In Damascus, they are also a favorite hobby and a type of competition. On rooftops throughout Damascus, young men keep coops filled with pigeons. In the after-noon, the young men head up to the roofs and release their flocks. They hope that their pigeons will lure pigeons from a different flock into their own. The men compete to see who can gather the largest flocks.

Syria's Nature Reserves

About 3 percent of the land in Syria has been set aside as protected areas. This is a low percentage compared to many other countries. Syria's largest protected area is Abd al-Aziz Mountain Reserve. It covers 207,688 acres (84,050 hectares) in the northeast. Pistachio and fruit trees thrive in Abd al-Aziz. Flowers such as gladiolus and tulips are also found in this reserve. Many kinds of animals make Abd al-Aziz their home, including foxes, wild cats, golden eagles, and vultures. Twenty-six endangered species also live there, including the gray wolf, the striped hyena, the badger, the Nubian ibex, and the short-toed eagle.

Golden eagles can have wingspans of up to 7 feet (2 m).

Red foxes are protected at the Fronloq Reserve.

Most other nature reserves in Syria are along the coast or near Syria's large cities in the west. Three sections of the Fronloq Reserve near Latakia have been set aside to protect pine and oak trees. Many types of wild animals live in this reserve, including cranes, Syrian woodpeckers, wolves, deer, and red foxes. Three other reserves near Latakia protect cedar, fir, and pine trees. Southeast of Aleppo, the Sabkhat Jabbul Nature Reserve is a rare protected wetland. A salt lake that attracts waterbirds is the main feature of this reserve.

A man looks over a narrow stretch of green along the Barada River.

Syria faces several environmental problems. Pollution is a serious problem. Syrians do not have enough clean drinking water. Many rivers, streams, and wells are polluted with raw sewage and waste from industry. Syria's coastline is polluted by waste from ships.

In addition, most of Syria's forests have been cut down to make room for fields, orchards, and expanding towns and cities. This has occurred mainly along the coast and in north-western Syria. Where the steppe and the Syrian Desert meet, overgrazing has occurred. Cattle, sheep, and goats have stripped whole areas of grass and shrubs. Without plant life to hold it in place, the fertile soil washes away. This erosion has caused parts of the steppe to become desert. In other words, the desert is growing.

Syria has taken steps to solve these problems. The Ministry of Environmental Affairs has started programs that should make Syria's air, water, and land cleaner and healthier both for people and animals. Syria's government has also signed several international agreements to protect the environment. These agreements deal with issues such as protecting wetlands and endangered species.

Syria's government has spent about $10 million on programs to upgrade factories so that they do not pollute the air and water. The government has also set up sewage and waste management projects in many cities. To halt soil erosion and the expansion of the desert, the Ministry of Agriculture has begun planting trees between the desert and the steppe. This "green belt" now extends from Dara in the south to the border with Turkey in the north.

Syrians take pride in these efforts when they celebrate Environment Day each October 14. They take every opportunity they can to enjoy the trees, flowers, and animals that still grow and live in their country.

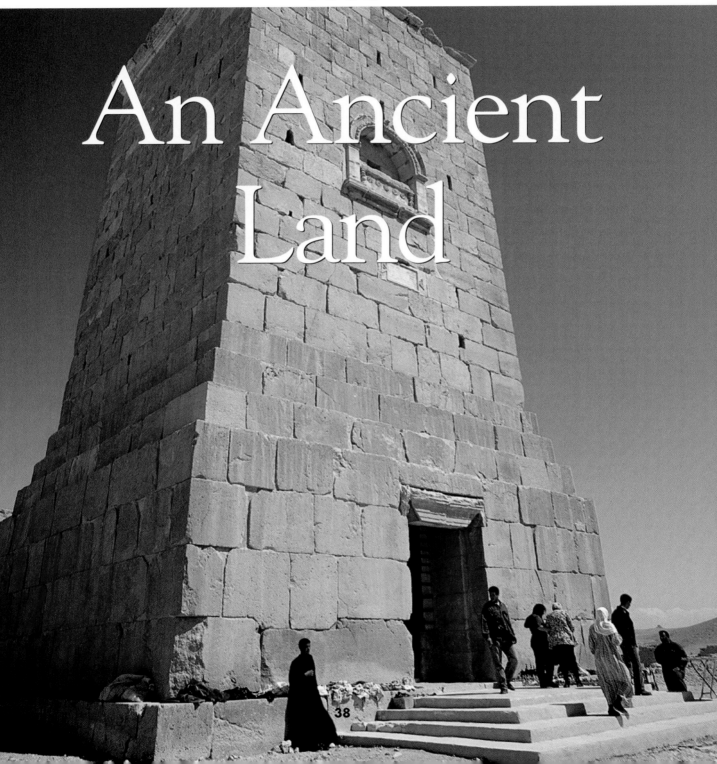

An Ancient Land

YRIA HAS ALWAYS BEEN A CROSSROADS. FOR THOUSANDS of years, its location and fertile land have attracted wandering nomads and well-equipped armies. Traders crossed this land as well, bringing goods from faraway China and India.

For most of its history, Syria has been surrounded by powerful neighbors. The kingdoms and empires of ancient Mesopotamia stood to the east. Powerful groups frequently invaded from the north in what is now Turkey. Threats also came from Egypt far to the south. Syria was often the prize in wars between these neighboring groups.

Opposite: **This tower in Palmyra dates back to ancient times. It was used for burial purposes.**

The first people in Syria settled along the Euphrates River.

Early People in Syria

People have been living in Syria for 150,000 years. Tools and weapons dating from that time have been found near Latakia on the coast and Mari on the Euphrates River. These ancient people hunted animals and lived in caves. By about 8000 B.C., people in Syria had developed agriculture. They planted grains and grew grapes. They also lived

in houses. Scientists have found the remains of houses with several rooms dating from this time in Mureybet. These artifacts show that Mureybet was one of the world's earliest villages.

Between 3500 B.C. and 1800 B.C., several cities were founded in Syria. Damascus and Aleppo were founded about 3000 B.C. Another city, Ebla, was founded about 3500 B.C. But unlike Damascus and Aleppo, it did not survive. In 1975, archaeologists found the ancient city of Ebla. The most important artifacts they found among the remains there were 17,000 clay tablets with cuneiform writing that date to about 2400 B.C. Cuneiform writing uses wedge-shaped characters. Each character is a word. From these clay tablets, historians learned that Ebla traded with Egypt and Mesopotamia and that people in Ebla made textiles. The city of Mari on the Euphrates River flourished around the same time as Ebla. In Mari, scientists have found 20,000 clay tablets written in cuneiform that date to about 1800 B.C.

The city of Ugarit developed on Syria's northwest coast. Clay tablets left there by people called the Phoenicians date to about 1300 B.C. These tablets were different from the earlier ones. Instead of being written in cuneiform, they were written using thirty symbols. Those symbols became the basis of the alphabet used in most countries today. The change from cuneiforms to letters made it much easier for people to learn to read and write.

This cuneiform tablet from Ugarit dates from about 1400 B.C.

During these early cen-
turies, large numbers of
people migrated to Syria
from neighboring lands.
About 2400 B.C., Sargon of
Akkad, which was located
in what is now Iraq, took
control of Syria, creating
the world's first empire.
About 2200 B.C., the
Amorites, another group
from what is now Iraq,
gained control of northern
Syria. The center of their
kingdom was Aleppo.
Later, the Mitanni and
then the Hittites con-
trolled the north. At the
same time, Egyptians con-
trolled the south. Hebrews

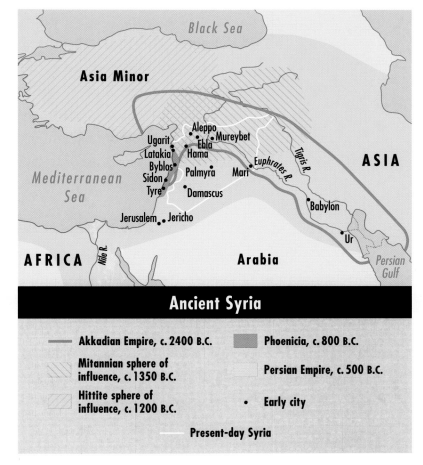

also moved north into Syria. Later still, the Aramaeans came
up from what is now Saudi Arabia. They settled in central and
northern Syria. The Aramaeans built the Citadel in Aleppo
and a temple to their god Baal-Haddad in Damascus. During
this period, the Aramaic language was adopted throughout
Syria. Between 732 B.C. and 539 B.C., Syria was again under
the rule of people from what is now Iraq—first by the
Assyrians and then by the Babylonians.

When Cyrus the Great of Persia (what is now Iran) defeated the Babylonians in 539 B.C., he made Syria a province of the Persian Empire. Syria had its own local government but paid taxes to the empire. Throughout the empire, the Persians built roads, issued coins, and adopted Aramaic as their official language. The Phoenician cities on the Syrian coast flourished. They provided ships for the Persians to use both for trade and for war with Egypt and Greece.

Greek, Roman, and Byzantine Rule

In 332 B.C., Alexander the Great of Greece conquered the Persian Empire. He left Syria under the control of his general Seleucus. Seleucus and his descendants, known as the Seleucids, ruled Syria for more than 200 years. Under their rule, trade expanded to India, China, and Europe. Greek ideas about law, philosophy, and science also took hold in Syria. By the 100s B.C., however, the Seleucids had become weak, and Syria was disorganized.

In 64 B.C., the Roman general Pompey marched into this weakened state. He made Syria a Roman province. Eventually, all of what is now the Middle East came under Roman rule. In Syria, the Romans built new roads, which increased the flow of trade. They also built aqueducts that carried water to cities and fields. In Bosra, the Romans built a huge amphitheater that is still used today. But Syria also had some influence on Rome. Four Syrians became Roman emperors.

During Roman rule, Christianity was born in Palestine in what is now Israel. This new religion quickly spread to Syria

and other parts of the Roman Empire. Before the coming of Christianity, Syrians practiced a variety of religions. Some worshipped gods of nature. Others worshipped the Roman gods. Still others practiced Judaism, the religion of the Hebrew people.

In A.D. 313, the Roman emperor Constantine declared Christianity to be the empire's official religion. Then, in 334, he moved the capital from Rome to Constantinople in Byzantium, now called Turkey. Trade flourished, and most Syrians enjoyed prosperity. But little by little, Byzantine rule grew weak in Syria. By the late 500s, Persians occupied part of Syria.

More tourists visit the Roman theater in Bosra than any other site in Syria.

The Arab Conquest

In the 620s and 630s, Muhammad, the prophet of Islam who lived in what is now Saudi Arabia, began spreading a new religion called Islam. After his death in 632, Muhammad's followers continued his work. In 633–634, a follower of Muhammad named Khalid ibn al-Walid led an invasion of Syria. By 635, he had gained control of Damascus. The Byzantine emperor Heraclius tried to repel the Arabs, but he was defeated.

Muhammad was born in Mecca, in what is now Saudi Arabia.

In 639, Muawiya of the Umayyad family became the governor of Syria. He gained the trust of newly arrived Muslim Arabs, as well as of Syria's Christian Arabs. In 661, Muawiya became caliph, or leader, of all the Muslims. He founded the Umayyad Dynasty and made Damascus its capital. By the time of his death, the Arab Muslim empire reached from present-day Afghanistan to present-day Algeria.

Under the Umayyads, Arabic replaced Aramaic as the spoken language in Syria, and many Syrians converted to Islam. The Umayyads built hospitals and schools, and Damascus became a center of learning. By 750, the Umayyads had become weak, and the Abbasid Dynasty gained control of the Muslim Empire. They moved the capital to Baghdad in present-day Iraq. Syria was again reduced to a province.

By 1000, Muslim control of Syria was split. But soon the Muslims would be united in fighting a common enemy. In 1098, Christians from Europe began the Crusades, a series of wars in which they tried to wrest control of the Holy Land (Palestine) from the Muslims. The Holy Land contained places connected to the life of Jesus.

At first, the European Crusaders were successful because the Muslim states were disorganized. The Crusaders marched through Syria and took control of a castle called the Crac des Chevalier. From this castle and other castles, they fought Arab Muslims. In 1099, the Crusaders took Jerusalem, killing almost all the Muslims and Jews in that city. During the Second Crusade, a Kurd named Salah ad-Din led Muslim forces against the Crusaders and regained Jerusalem. Salah ad-Din united Syria with Egypt under his Ayyubid Dynasty. Syria enjoyed peace and prosperity under the Ayyubids.

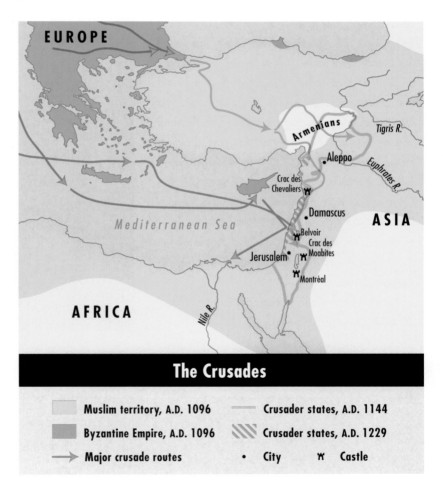

EUROPE

Armenians

Tigris R.

Aleppo

Euphrates R.

Crac des Chevaliers

Damascus

ASIA

Mediterranean Sea

Belvoir
Crac des Moabites

Jerusalem

Montréal

AFRICA

Nile R.

The Crusades

Muslim territory, A.D. 1096   Crusader states, A.D. 1144

Byzantine Empire, A.D. 1096   Crusader states, A.D. 1229

Major crusade routes   • City   Castle

Salah ad-Din

Salah ad-Din was one of the world's most skillful military leaders. He is one of the greatest heroes of the Muslim world. Even the Christian Crusaders he fought against considered him a brave and honorable man and a brilliant military strategist.

Salah ad-Din was born in 1138 into a Kurdish family. He grew up in the court of Nur al-Din, the leader who had unified the Muslim states to fight the Christian Crusaders. Salah Ad-Din had his first great military success in the 1160s, defending Egypt from the Crusaders. He eventually united Syria and Egypt under his rule.

In 1187, he led Muslim armies that defeated the Crusaders, recapturing Jerusalem from the Christians. When the Christians had taken control of Jerusalem in 1099, they had slaughtered almost all the Jews and Muslims in the city. But when Salah ad-Din recaptured it, he allowed the city's Christians to leave peacefully. In 1192, Salah ad-Din and King Richard the Lion-Hearted of England made a truce that gave Christians control of the coast and allowed them to visit their holy shrines in Jerusalem.

Salah ad-Din died in Damascus in 1193. He is buried at the Umayyad Mosque.

From Mamelukes to Ottomans

In 1250, the Mameluke Dynasty from Egypt took over from the Ayyubids. The Mamelukes forced the last of the Crusaders out of Syria and the Holy Land in 1302. Under Mameluke rule, Damascus grew in importance. Syrian Arabs gained government positions. Seagoing merchants from Europe traded along Syria's coast. Prosperity lasted until 1401, when invaders from the east burned Aleppo and Damascus. For the next hundred years, Syria experienced a great decline.

While Syria was weakening, the Ottoman Empire, which was based in Turkey to the north, was gaining strength. In 1516, the Ottomans invaded Syria, defeating the Mamelukes in Aleppo. From Syria, they expanded their empire to include most of the Muslim world.

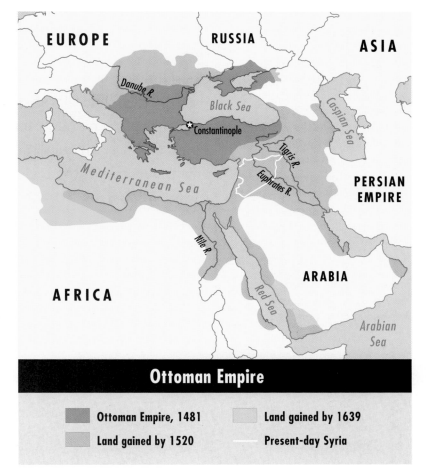

Now that the Ottomans had power, Syria was again treated as a province. Aleppo developed as a destination for European traders. On the whole, though, Syria's economy was stagnant under Ottoman rule. The population decreased, with entire villages disappearing. By the end of the 1700s, the Ottoman Empire itself was in decline. It took another hundred years and a world war before it totally collapsed.

By the 1800s, the Ottoman Turks feared the great empires of Austria-Hungary and Russia that had developed along their northern border. The Ottomans turned to Britain and France for help, accepting money, weapons, and training. Both countries saw Syria as an important trading center, and France became influential in the region.

Meanwhile, many Syrians began to think about independence from the Ottomans. Other Arabs in the Middle East also began clamoring for independence. Then, in 1914, World War I broke out. In this war, France, Britain, and Russia were fighting Germany and Austria-Hungary. By this time, the Ottomans were relying on Germany for support, so they joined

In the nineteenth century, the French became actively involved in Syrian affairs.

Germany in the war. The British encouraged Arabs seeking self-rule to revolt against the Ottomans. On May 6, 1916, some of the rebels were hanged in Damascus. But Prince Faisal ibn Hussein of Saudi Arabia continued to lead Arabs from throughout the Middle East in a revolt against the Turks. In October 1918, the Arab forces took Damascus.

Prince Faisal with various delegates and advisors in 1919

The following month, World War I ended with the defeat of Germany and the Ottoman Empire. In 1919, Prince Faisal declared Syria a free and independent country. At this time, Syria also included Lebanon, Jordan, and Palestine. But instead of independence, Syria was divided between France and Britain. Palestine and Jordan went to Britain. Syria and Lebanon came under French rule.

Britain and France were supposed to prepare these areas for self-government. Instead France treated Syria like a colony. French became the language used in schools, and the French national anthem was sung there. But Syrians continued to work for independence, and the French put down several revolts. After World War II ended, the French were convinced to withdraw from Syria. In 1946, French troops finally left the country. Syria was at last an independent nation.

An Ancient Land **49**

Syria wasn't the only Middle Eastern country created at this time. The United Nations decided to divide Palestine into an Arab state and a Jewish state. The Jewish state became known as Israel. In 1948, Syria, Jordan, and Egypt went to war with the young state of Israel. They wanted to stop the partition from occurring. When the war ended in 1949, Syria had gained a small slice of land around Lake Tiberias. But the other Arab countries had failed to stop the partition. The end of this war marked the beginning of the Arab-Israeli conflict that continues to this day. Syria's poor showing in the war cost President Shukri al-Quwatli his job. He was overthrown by army officers. This began the military's intervention in Syria's government.

In the 1950s, Syria faced many problems. For example, about 1 percent of the population owned more than 50 percent of the land. The government's efforts to make land ownership more fair failed. Syria's weak government was unable to solve the country's problems. So Syrians looked to Egypt for help. In 1958, the two countries combined to form the United Arab Republic (UAR). Syria was not treated as an equal in this partnership, however, so in 1961, it pulled out of the UAR. One success of the UAR was a land reform program that the Syrian government continued to carry out into the late 1960s.

The Baath Party played an important part in carrying out the land reforms. *Baath* means "rebirth." The Baaths wanted a rebirth of Arab unity and freedom. The party members also wanted socialism—they thought the government should control the economy through ownership of factories, mines, and other means of production. On March 8, 1963, the Baath Party and army officers seized control of the government. Since then, the Baath has been Syria's most powerful political party.

In 1967, Israel fought Egypt, Jordan, and Syria in the Six-Day War. The Arab countries went down in defeat, with Israel grabbing a bit of land from each of them. Syria lost the Golan Heights. Return of the Golan remains Syria's condition for a lasting peace treaty with Israel.

Israeli troops return home to cheers after their victory in the Six-Day War.

Hafiz al-Asad took control of
Syria in 1970.

Syria Under the Asads

By 1970, Syria had experienced nine changes in government
in twenty-five years, five of them military coups. That year,
Hafiz al-Asad, a Baath Party member and a military officer,
seized power and held it for thirty years. Al-Asad was able to
keep power because he brought other political parties together
with the Baath to form the National Progressive Front. He
also had complete control of the Baath Party and of the
military. Al-Asad put through programs for economic development, land reform, and improved education. But he did not
allow Syrians to speak freely or exercise their rights, and he
violently put down protests.

Al-Asad also had problems with other countries. In 1975,
Egypt and Syria went to war against Israel. Syria regained a

small slice of the Golan Heights, but most of the Golan remained in Israel's control. Then in 1976, al-Asad sent troops to resolve Lebanon's civil war. Although the civil war ended in 1990, Syria remained in Lebanon.

Al-Asad remained in power until his death in 2000. Then his son Bashar al-Asad became president. Bashar seemed open to reforms. People were able to speak more freely. They felt they could give advice to the government on how to bring about democracy in Syria. But by early 2001, the government had already cracked down on the reformers. Their groups were broken up. Some writers were beaten. Other reformers were thrown into prison. Although Bashar might be willing to look at government reforms, the old-time leaders of the Baath Party don't want to give up their power. For now, at least, political change seems slow in coming.

Syria's Leaders Since Independence

President Shukri al-Quwatli, 1946–1949

General Husni al-Zaim, March 1949–August 1949

General Sami al-Hinnawi, August 1949–December 1949

Colonel Adib Shishakli, December 1949–February 1954

President Shukri al-Quwatli, 1955–1958

Gamal Abdul Nasser of Egypt, president of the United Arab Republic, 1958–1961

(Abdul Hakim of Syria acted as supervisor in Syria)

President Nazim al-Qudsi, 1961–1963

General Amin al-Hafiz, 1963–1966

President Salah al-Jadid, 1966–1970

President Hafiz al-Asad, 1970–2000

President Bashar al-Asad, 2000–present

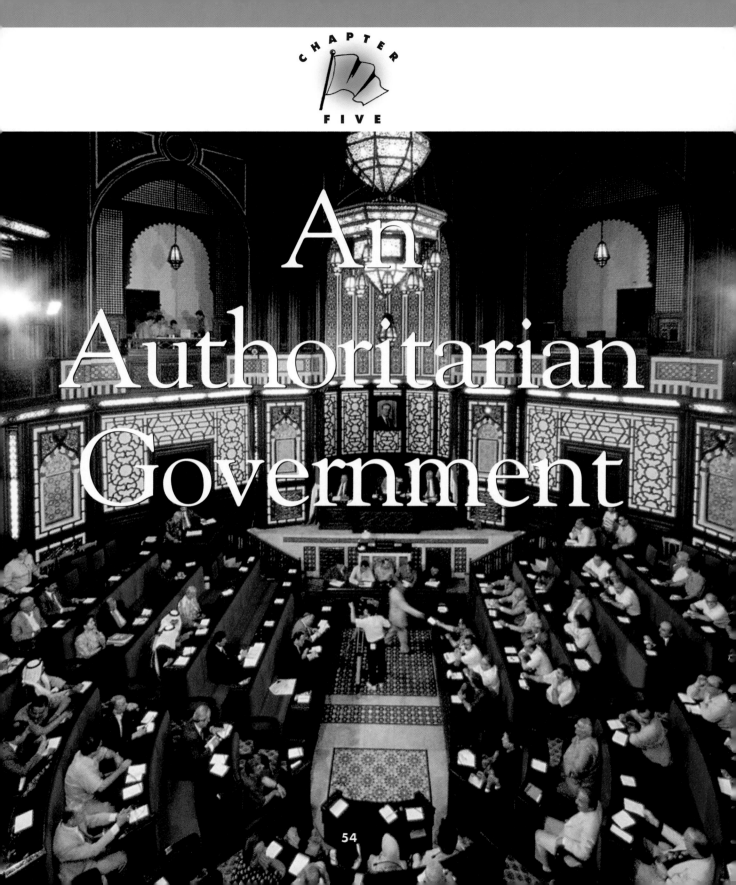

An Authoritarian Government

S INCE HAFIZ AL-ASAD CAME TO POWER IN 1970, SYRIA'S government has been marked by one-man, one-party rule backed by a strong military. All governmental power is controlled by the president. In the late 1970s and early 1980s, a group called the Muslim Brotherhood fought al-Asad's rule. They set off bombs and killed government officials. The government responded by killing thousands of people in an effort to stop the uprising.

Since that time, Syria has officially been in a "state of emergency." The government has used this as an excuse to restrict people's civil rights and political freedoms. Since 2000, President Bashar al-Asad has allowed more freedom of

Opposite: **The Syrian parliament**

Syria's Flag

Syria's flag is made of three equal bands of red, white, and black. Red represents Syria's struggle for freedom; white stands for peace; and black symbolizes Syria's colonial past. The two green stars stand for Syria and Egypt, the two countries of the United Arab Republic (UAR). This was Syria's flag during the years of the UAR. In 1961, Syria withdrew from the UAR. In 1980, however, this flag was re-adopted as Syria's national flag.

speech and freedom of the press. But Syrians still fear the eyes and ears of the secret police.

Syria's government is authoritarian, meaning that power is held by just a few people. Like most authoritarian governments, Syria's government is corrupt. Syrian officials often demand bribes from citizens for ordinary services.

Nevertheless, Syria has the framework for a freer government. Syria's constitution, adopted in 1973, says the country is a democratic, popular, socialist republic. The constitution also guarantees freedom of speech, press, and assembly.

A Strong Presidency

Syria's government has three branches—executive, legislative, and judicial. Although this sounds similar to the United States government, it isn't. Syria's president controls all three branches of government. A candidate for president must be an Arab and a Muslim. Until 2000, a presidential candidate also had to be forty years old. In 2000, the constitution was changed so that thirty-four-year-old Bashar al-Asad could become president. Once elected, the president serves for a term of seven years, and there is no limit to the number of terms one person can serve.

The Asad Dynasty

Hafiz al-Asad (1930–2000) (right) was born in Qardaha into a farming family. His given name was Abu Sulayman. When he was about fifteen years old, he changed his name to Hafiz al-Asad, which means "the Lion's Guard." Later in life, he was known as "the Lion of Damascus." Hafiz was a good student. He attended secondary school in Latakia, where he organized a Baath Party student group in 1947. After graduating, he served as a pilot in Syria's air force.

Meanwhile, Hafiz was moving up the ladder in the Baath Party. In 1963, he helped bring about the successful Baath revolution. He soon became minister of defense and commander of Syria's air force. Using his influence in the Baath Party and in the military, Hafiz seized power in 1970. He became president in 1971. In the 1980s, he began preparing his oldest son, Basil, to succeed him as president. But in 1994, Basil was killed in an automobile accident. Hafiz then started preparing his second son, Bashar, to be president.

Bashar al-Asad (left) was born in Damascus in 1965. When his brother died, Bashar was an ophthalmologist in London, England, with no interest in politics. To prepare for Syria's presidency, Bashar moved back to Syria. He began military training and by 1999 was a colonel. He also represented his father on trips to other countries. Besides Arabic, Bashar speaks fluent English and French. He is interested in computer technology and the Internet, and has headed Syria's Computer Society since 1994.

Since being installed as Syria's president on July 17, 2000, Bashar has made attempts to crack down on corruption. He has also allowed Syrians a bit more freedom. In addition, Bashar is trying to build political and economic ties with other parts of the world.

Syria's president is also the commander in chief of the armed services. In addition, the president is the chair of the Baath Party. The president appoints two vice presidents, a prime minister, all the ministers in the cabinet, and the members of the Supreme Constitutional Court. He can also dismiss these officials.

Syria's president also tells the legislature what laws to pass. He can dissolve the legislature and call for new elections. The legislative branch is made up of the People's Council, or Majlis al Shaab. Every four years, 250 Syrians are elected to the People's Council. The members of the council pass laws and approve treaties sent to them by the president.

Bashar al-Asad speaks before the Syrian parliament.

The judicial system is also under the president's control. Syria's judicial system has many layers of courts. The High Judicial Council, chaired by Syria's president, appoints and dismisses judges on all the other courts. The High Constitutional Court, also chaired by the president, rules on disputed elections and the constitutionality of Syria's laws. The Supreme State Security Court tries national security cases. The Economic

NATIONAL GOVERNMENT OF SYRIA

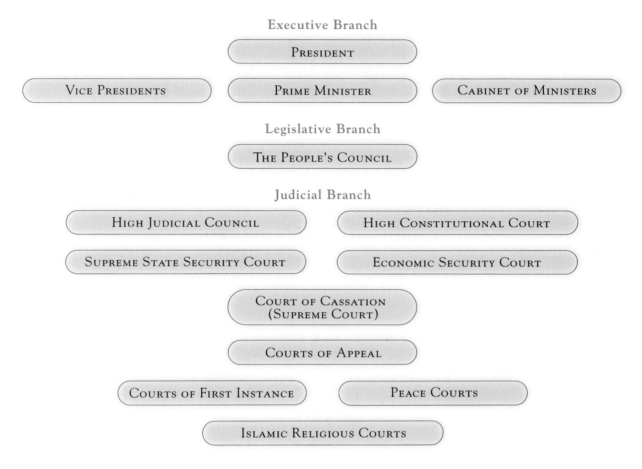

Executive Branch

PRESIDENT

VICE PRESIDENTS   PRIME MINISTER   CABINET OF MINISTERS

Legislative Branch

THE PEOPLE'S COUNCIL

Judicial Branch

HIGH JUDICIAL COUNCIL   HIGH CONSTITUTIONAL COURT

SUPREME STATE SECURITY COURT   ECONOMIC SECURITY COURT

COURT OF CASSATION
(SUPREME COURT)

COURTS OF APPEAL

COURTS OF FIRST INSTANCE   PEACE COURTS

ISLAMIC RELIGIOUS COURTS

Security Court tries cases involving financial crimes. Syria's supreme court is the Court of Cassation. Under it are Courts of Appeal that hear appeals either on civil or criminal cases. The courts where cases start are called Courts of First Instance and Peace Courts. Syria also has religious courts that take care of matters of Islamic law. These courts mostly hear matters that concern children, marriage, divorce, and inheritance.

Regional and Local Government

In addition to Syria's central government, the nation has thirteen district governments called *mouhafazats*. Each district has the same name as its capital city, and its government is headed by a governor. Each district also has a council and civil and criminal courts of appeal. Towns and villages have governments made up of a mayor and elected municipal councils.

The main task of regional and local governments is to collect taxes. Local government policies are handed down from the Ministry of the Interior in Damascus.

The Baath Party

The main power in Syria resides in the Baath Party. Its place as the country's leading party is stated in the constitution. The Baath Party controls the military and the secret police. Its main goal is to build a strong Arab socialist state. The Baath believe that people should be loyal to the nation rather than to an ethnic or religious group.

In 1972, the Baath Party formed the National Progressive Front (NPF). The NPF is made up of the Baath Party and five smaller parties. Two-thirds of the seats in the national legislature are set aside for NPF candidates. The rest of the seats go to candidates from a few independent parties.

The Military

The military plays a large role in Syrian life. Syria considers itself in a state of war because of the long-standing conflict with Israel. Syria spends about 10 percent of its gross domestic product on defense. This is much more than the average for countries around the world, which is just 2.6 percent. Some of that money pays for Syria's defense forces.

At the age of eighteen, all Syrian men must serve in the military for two years. Currently, about 215,000 men serve in Syria's army, about 4,000 are in the navy, and about 40,000 are in the air force. In an emergency, the government can also call on about 280,000 army reservists. Additional money is spent on military equipment such as ships, guns, aircraft, and helicopters.

All Syrian men must serve in the military.

The Secret Police

While Syria's military protects Syria from outside threats, the *mukhabarat*, or secret police, protects the government from Syrian citizens. About 65,000 full-time mukhabarat and several hundred thousand part-time mukhabarat spy on Syrians at work, at school, on the street, and in restaurants.

Syrians are careful about what they say or do in public. By speaking out against the president, a Syrian could easily become a political prisoner. At one time, several thousand Syrians were held and tortured in prisons. Today, a few hundred Syrians remain in prison for political acts.

Foreign Policy

For the most part, the Arab-Israeli conflict has determined Syria's foreign policy. Because of the ongoing battles, the country has built a strong military. More recently, Syrian leaders have taken part in talks with Israel in an effort to regain the Golan Heights.

Syria continues to play a role in Lebanese politics. In 2004, Syria encouraged the Lebanese government to change its constitution to allow its pro-Syria president to serve more terms. In 2005, a former Lebanese prime minister who was anti-Syrian was assassinated. Syria denied having anything to do with his death, but many people believed Syria was behind it. In 2005, Syria withdrew its troops from Lebanon because of pressure from other countries and from the United Nations.

Syria maintains close ties with Russia. In 2005, Russia canceled $9.8 billion of the debt owed by Syria. Relations

between Syria and the United States are tense at best. Various Palestinian extremist groups operate out of Syria. These groups carry out attacks within Israel. Because of Syria's connections with terrorists, the United States has placed trade sanctions on Syria. Only food and medicine can be imported into Syria from the United States. No goods can be exported from Syria to the United States.

Syrian troops withdraw from Lebanon in 2005.

Damascus: Did You Know This?

Damascus sits on the Barada River in the shadow of Mount Qassioun. People have lived in Damascus for more than 5,000 years. It is one of the world's oldest continuously inhabited cities. Damascus has been the capital since Syria became independent in 1946. In 2004, Damascus was Syria's second-largest city, with a population of 1,700,000. The city has an average January temperature of 38°F (3.4°C) and an average July temperature of 77°F (25.2°C). Annual rainfall averages 8.8 inches (22 cm).

The people of Damascus are proud of their city's historic sites. A few of the most famous sites in the Old City are the Umayyad Mosque, the Umayyad Souq, and the Azem Palace. Sites from Damascus's

Christian history include Straight Street, the Chapel of Ananias, and Saint Paul's Chapel (left). Martyrs' Square, the Hejaz Train Station (above), and the National Museum are highlights in central Damascus. Among Damascus's important government buildings are the Presidential Palace, the domed Parliament building, and the Palace of Justice.

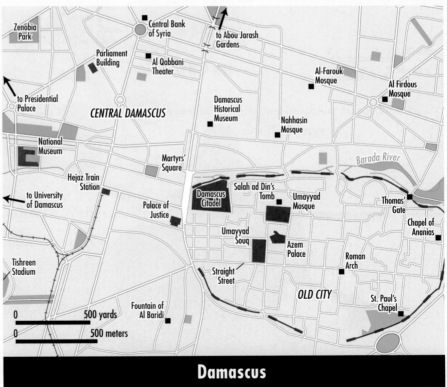

Zenobia Park

to Presidential Palace

Parliament Building

National Museum

Hejaz Train Station

to University of Damascus

Tishreen Stadium

Central Bank of Syria

Al Qabbani Theater

to Abou Jarash Gardens

CENTRAL DAMASCUS

Damascus Historical Museum

Al-Farouk Mosque

Al Firdous Mosque

Nahhasin Mosque

Martyrs' Square

Barada River

Palace of Justice

Damascus Citadel

Salah ad Din's Tomb

Umayyad Mosque

Thomas Gate

Chapel of Ananias

Umayyad Souq

Azem Palace

Roman Arch

Straight Street

OLD CITY

St. Paul's Chapel

Fountain of Al Baridi

0   500 yards

0   500 meters

Damascus

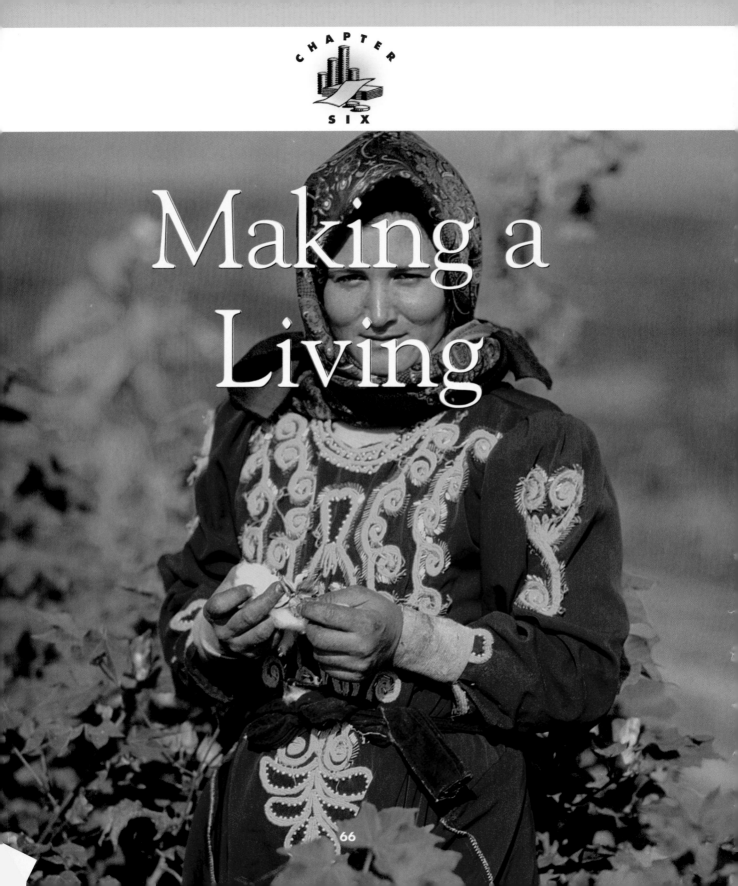

Making a Living

S YRIA'S ECONOMY FACES MANY PROBLEMS. THE GOVERNment controls most of Syria's economy, but government regulation has held back development. Somewhere between 20 percent and 65 percent of Syrians live in poverty. The country has a high rate of population growth, and about 60 percent of its people are under 20 years of age. Its industries are not growing at a rate that keeps up with population growth. As a result, Syria suffers from high unemployment. At least 25 percent of the adults are out of work. Although about 33 percent of the workforce is engaged in farming, Syria doesn't grow enough food crops to feed itself. Syria also has a weak banking system and no stock market.

Opposite: **A woman picks cotton**

Syrian Currency

Syria's official unit of currency is the Syrian pound (SYP), also called the *lira*. Syrian coins come in dominations

of 1, 2, 5, 10, and 25 SYPs. Banknote denominations are 50, 100, 200, 500, and 1,000 SYPs. In 2005, the exchange rate was one U.S. dollar equals 51.9 SYP.

Syria's colorful banknotes reflect the nation's rich history. People and buildings from Syrian history are shown on the front of the notes. They include rulers such as former President Hafiz al-Asad and buildings such as the Crac des Chevaliers. The backs of the banknotes feature elements of the modern economy, such as dams, oil refineries, and Syrians working in agriculture and manufacturing.

What a Syrian Pound (SYP) Can Buy

Item	Cost in Syrian Pounds	Cost in U.S. Dollars
Fresh fruit juice drink	30 SYP	$0.60
Meat sandwich	75 SYP	$1.50
Souvenir T-shirt	500 SYP	$10.00
Shirt or blouse	700–800 SYP	$14.00–16.00
Slacks	600–900 SYP	$12.00–18.00
1 liter (2.6 gallons) of gasoline	6.85 SYP	$0.14
Old used car	100,000 SYP	$2,000.00
Newer used car	500,000 SYP	$10,000.00
Used bicycle	2,000 SUP	$40.00

The government has begun to address some of these problems. In 2004, four privately owned banks opened, and a committee was formed to set up a stock market. The government is also allowing more private enterprise.

Agriculture

About 30 percent of Syria's land is good for farming. Most of the farmland lies in the northeast and northwest and along the Orontes and Euphrates rivers. Dams on the rivers provide water for irrigating nearby fields. When the Orontes River is high enough, the waterwheels in Hama lift water up to irrigation canals that carry the water to the fields. Most Syrian farmers own their own farms. The government runs a few very large farms.

Syria's most important cash crops are wheat, barley, sugar beets, and cotton. Northeastern Syria has groves of orange, lemon, and lime trees. Apple, cherry, apricot, and peach trees also grow there. Trees bearing olives, figs, and almonds also provide important crops. Syria is one of the world's leading producers of olives. Many vegetable crops are grown in Syria, including chickpeas, lentils, cabbages, lettuce, tomatoes, pumpkins, squash, cucumbers, eggplants, onions, and peppers.

A Syrian farmer plows a field.

The Cotton Festival

Cotton was Syria's most valuable export until the 1980s, when oil surpassed it. Cotton still remains an important crop in Syria. Each year at the end of the cotton harvest, Aleppo hosts the Cotton Festival. Most of Syria's cotton is grown near Aleppo, and many tex-

tile plants in that city produce cotton cloth. During the festival, Syrians give thanks for the current crop and pray for good weather for the next year's crop. They also make noise to keep locusts away from the cotton fields.

Raising livestock is also important to Syrian agriculture. The country's farmers raise about 21 million chickens each year. Bedouins raise most of the sheep, goats, cattle, horses,

Syrians raise goats on the dry grasslands.

What Syria Grows, Makes, and Mines	
Agriculture (2001)	
Wheat	4,744,600 metric tons
Barley	1,955,600 metric tons
Sugar beets	1,215,500 metric tons
Manufacturing	
Fuel oil (1999)	10,629,000 metric tons
Cement (2001)	5,428,000 metric tons
Cottonseed cake (2001)	281,000 metric tons
Mining (2001)	
Phosphate rock	2,043,000 metric tons
Gypsum	345,000 metric tons
Crude oil	194,000 metric tons

mules, and camels. They move herds of these animals from place to place in search of grazing land. Sheep are Syria's most important livestock. They provide meat, milk, and wool for cloth.

Mining

Oil is Syria's most important mineral product. But compared with the oil-rich countries of the Middle East, Syria's oil deposits are small. Syria's five oil fields are located in the northeast. The oil in these fields is expected to run out by about 2010. Syria also has reserves of natural gas. Currently, natural gas is used in place of oil for generating power because the government wants to sell oil as an export.

Phosphate rock is another important Syrian mineral. Most of the phosphate mines are in the area around Palmyra. Phosphate is used in making fertilizer. Most of Syria's phosphate is exported to Europe. Other large mineral deposits include gypsum, salt, and marble. Gypsum is used to make wallboard for the interior of homes. Gypsum is also added to soil to make it more productive.

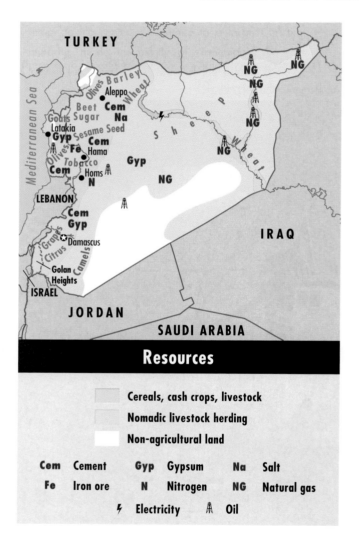

Resources

Cereals, cash crops, livestock

Nomadic livestock herding

Non-agricultural land

Cem	Cement	Gyp	Gypsum	Na	Salt
Fe	Iron ore	N	Nitrogen	NG	Natural gas
		⚡	Electricity	⛏	Oil

Manufacturing

Manufacturing is a growing part of Syria's economy. Oil is Syria's most important manufactured product. Fertilizer, ammonia, and refined oil are produced in Homs. Steel and iron goods come from plants in Hama. Syria's second most important manufactured product is cement. Plants in Tartus, Adra, Hama, and Aleppo produce most of the country's cement.

Textile mills in Aleppo, Damascus, Hama, and Homs produce cotton, nylon, and wool cloth. Natural silk is produced in Latakia. Sugar, olive oil, and cottonseed cake lead the list of Syria's refined food products. Other goods manufactured in Syria include refrigerators, washing machines, and television sets.

A factory worker makes television sets in Damascus.

Trade and Tourism

Syria's service industries account for 53 percent of the country's economy. Trade and tourism are leading service industries in Syria. Trade is a vital part of Syria's economy. In early 2005, Syria signed a free-trade agreement with the European Union to enhance relations with its member countries. This agreement will make European goods available to Syrians at lower prices. Syria's main trading partners are China, France, Italy, Saudi Arabia, and Turkey. The main goods exported from Syria are oil and oil products, vegetables, fruits, and cotton. Syria's main imports include machinery, automobiles, trucks, processed foods, iron and steel, chemicals, and textile yarns.

Tourism is an increasingly important part of Syria's economy. It provides about 92,000 jobs in hotels, resorts, restaurants, national reserves, and historic attractions. Tourism also helps the construction industry. Each year, more luxury hotels are constructed in Damascus and Aleppo. Seaside resorts are booming in Latakia. In 2004, about 6 million tourists spent $1.8 billion in Syria. About 3 million of these travelers came from other Arab countries for extended stays. An additional 3 million travelers from nearby Jordan, Lebanon, Iraq, and Turkey came for one-day stays. Only about 300,000 Europeans and Americans visited Syria in 2004. Many visitors travel to the ancient ruins of Ugarit and Palmyra. They also enjoy touring the Crusader castles, historic palaces, mosques, and nature reserves.

Transportation

Syria's transportation system takes people anywhere from the beaches and mountains to the vast desert of Syria. It also allows raw materials and finished goods to be moved around, into, and out of Syria. The country's main airports are at Damascus, Aleppo, and Latakia. Syrian Arab Airlines is the national airline. Most of Syria's railroads are in the western part of the country. They link Syria's major cities and reach as far as Amman, Jordan, and Baghdad, Iraq, and several cities in Lebanon.

Most Syrians travel by car or bus. Syria has about 18,770 miles (30,200 km) of roads. Many Syrians use microbuses and minibuses to travel around the country. Microbuses travel between cities and have routes to small towns and villages. Minibuses travel on short routes between towns and villages. These buses do not have set schedules. Instead, they usually leave when they are full of passengers.

Syria's official system of weights and measures is the metric system. However, the traditional weight based on the *okiya* is sometimes still used. One okiya equals 0.47 pounds or 0.21 kilograms. Larger weights include the *oke*, which equals 6 okiyas (2.82 pounds or 1.27 kg).

Millions of tourists travel to Syria each year.

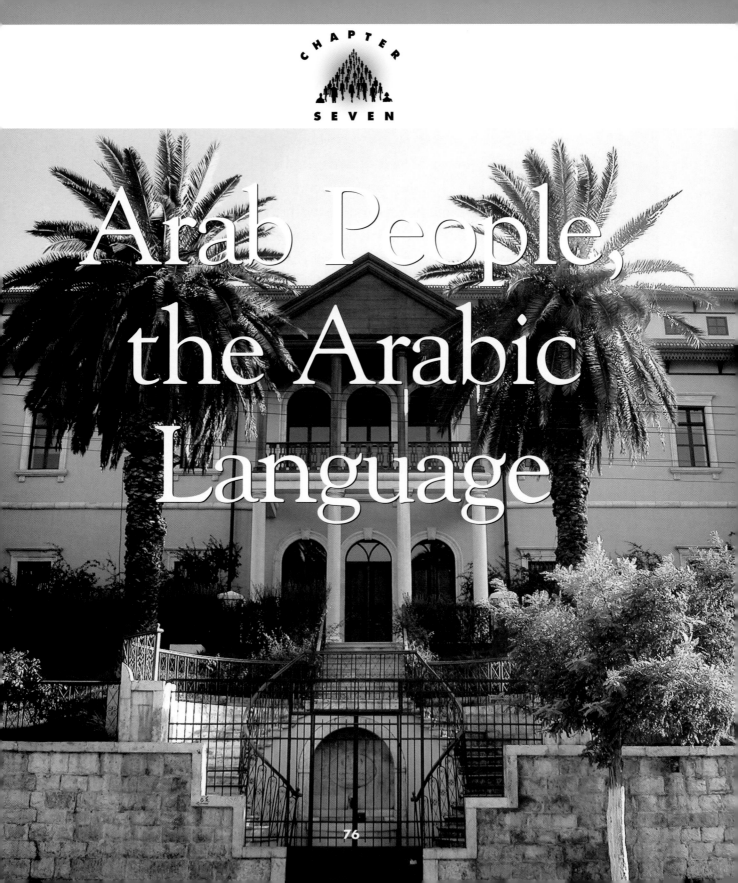

Arab People, the Arabic Language

M ANY DIFFERENT GROUPS MIGRATED TO SYRIA OVER the last 5,000 years. In most cases, these groups have mingled to become the Syrian people. The group with the greatest influence were the Muslim Arabs, who invaded in 633. Today, most Syrians are Arab, and they all speak Arabic.

In 2004, Syria had an estimated population of 19,230,000 people. That's a little more than the number of people who live in the state of New York. About 55 percent of Syrians live

Opposite: **Damascus University**

The souq in Damascus

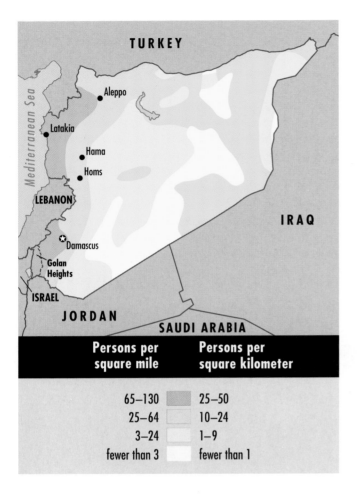

Persons per square mile	Persons per square kilometer
65–130	25–50
25–64	10–24
3–24	1–9
fewer than 3	fewer than 1

Population of Major Cities (2004 estimate)

Aleppo	2,000,000
Damascus	1,700,000
Homs	715,500
Latakia	303,000
Hama	273,000

in cities. But this number is rising. Every year, more Syrians leave the countryside and move to the cities. Syria's population is also very young. About 38 percent of the people are less than fifteen years of age. In the United States, only 21 percent of the people are under fifteen.

Syria averages about 269 people per square mile (103 persons per sq km). But Syrians are not spread out evenly across the country. Most people live along the seacoast and in the strip of cities and towns from Damascus to Aleppo. Many people also live in Syria's far northeastern triangle and in the southwestern corner. Few people live in the eastern steppe or in the Syrian Desert.

The People of Syria

Syria considers itself an Arab nation. The government tries to promote the idea of a united Arab culture, and it plays down differences between ethnic groups. Nevertheless, Syria is home to a number of different ethnic groups. About 90 percent of Syrians belong to the Arab ethnic group. They trace their heritage back to groups of people who migrated into Syria from what is now Saudi Arabia between about 1200 B.C.

and A.D. 640. Arabs live throughout Syria. Most Arabs follow the rules of Islam, and they all speak the Arabic language.

The word *Arab* comes from a term that means "to move around," which is what the early Arabs did. They were nomads who moved from place to place to find grazing land for their sheep and camels. About 100,000 Syrian Arabs still live this kind of life. They are Syria's Bedouins. Bedouins who are no longer nomads are known as sedentary Arabs. They have settled in Syria's towns and cities, where many of them work in construction or drive trucks.

Traditional Bedouin families live in tents that can be folded up and moved from place to place.

Most Syrian Kurds live in the northeastern part of the country.

Who Lives in Syria?

Arabs	90%
Kurds	9%
Armenians, Circassians, Turkomans	1%

Syria's largest non-Arab ethnic group is the Kurds. They make up about 9 percent of Syria's population. Like most of Syria's Arabs, most Kurds are Sunni Muslims. The Kurds, however, have their own language. Kurds have lived in Syria for about a thousand years. Syria's most famous Kurd was Salah ad-Din, the great military leader who defeated the Christian Crusaders. Today, most Kurds in Syria live in the northeast. Many Syrian Kurds would like this part of Syria to become part of an independent country, which they would call Kurdistan. Kurdistan would also take parts of Iraq, Iran, and Turkey.

Armenians, Circassians, and Turkomans also live in Syria. Together, they make up about 1 percent of the population. Armenians first came to Syria more than 2,500 years ago from eastern Europe. They settled mainly around Aleppo. During World War I, several thousand more Armenians fled Turkey and settled in Syria. The Armenians are Christians and have their own language. The Circassians are Sunni Muslims who came from southern Russia in the 1800s. Many of them live as farmers in the Hauran area. Others make their homes in

Armenians en route to Syria via the Mediterranean Sea in 1915

Damascus. The Turkomans are Sunni Muslims who came from central Asia. Most of them speak Arabic, but some still speak Turkish. Some Turkomans are semi-nomadic herders in northeastern Syria and along the southern Euphrates River. Others have become farmers near Aleppo.

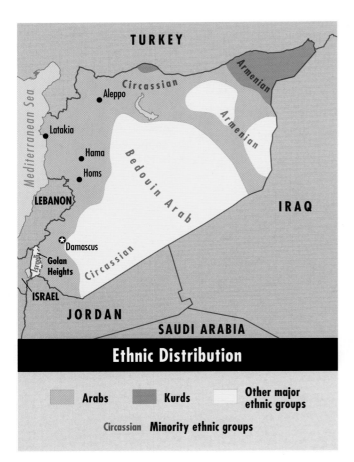

Ethnic Distribution

Arabs   Kurds   Other major ethnic groups

Circassian   Minority ethnic groups

Syria's Languages

Arabic is Syria's official language. All Syrians speak Arabic, even if they also speak the language of their ethnic group. Syria's Bedouins speak the purest form of Arabic. It is much like the language spoken by the Arabs who swept into Syria in the 630s. Called classical Arabic, this is the language in which the Quran is written. Modern Standard Arabic is the form used in Syria's schools, on radio and television, and in books and newspapers. Within Syria, several dialects, or versions, of Arabic are spoken. People in different cities and sometimes even in different neighborhoods speak distinct dialects.

Many members of Syria's ethnic groups speak a second language in addition to Arabic. At home and among friends, they speak the language of their own ethnic group. Armenian,

Turkish, and the Kurds' Kirmanji language are the most common second languages in Syria. The ancient language of Aramaic is still used in Maalula and the nearby villages of Bakha and Jabbadin. When France controlled Syria, French was the language of government, business, and education. French is still spoken by educated people in Syria's cities. It is also used for business transactions with other countries. English, however, is quickly becoming more popular than French as a second language in Syria's schools.

The Quran is written in classical Arabic.

The Arabic Alphabet

a	ا	d*	ض
b	ب	t*	ط
t	ت	z*	ظ
th	ث	a pause	ع
g	ج	gh	غ
h	ح	f	ف
kh	خ	q	ق
d	د	k	ك
dh	ذ	l	ل
r	ر	m	م
z	ز	n	ن
s	س	h	ه
sh	ش	w	و
s*	ص	y	ي

*Harder sounds than regular letters

Writing in Arabic can be an art form.

Written Arabic

Although spoken Arabic has many dialects, this language is written in only one way. The Arabic alphabet has twenty-eight letters. The letters have curves, loops, and horizontal lines. Some letters also have dots and geometric shapes. Each letter has more than one shape depending on whether it comes at the beginning, the middle, or the end of a word or if the letter stands alone.

Arabic is written from right to left and from top to bottom. Sometimes, Arabic is written in an elaborate calligraphy. This beautiful writing is considered a fine art.

Education

All public education in Syria is free, from elementary school all the way through college. In Syria, children are required to go to school from ages six to twelve. In elementary school, boys and girls attend classes together. All classes are taught in Arabic. During the third year of school, students must also study English or French. Most subjects are taught through memorization. Students are also taught to support the government, so they are not encouraged to think for themselves.

Common Arabic Words and Phrases

addaysh essa'aa?	What time is it?
'afwan	You're welcome
aiwa	Yes
bi addaysh?	How much is it?
la	No
kayf Haalak?	How are you?
ma'a salaama	Good-bye
marHaba	Hi
min fadlak	Please
shu-ismak?	What is your name?
shukran	Thank-you

Syrian Body Language

Syrians often use hand gestures and head motions in place of speech or to emphasize what they are saying. Here are some examples of Syrian body language:

Palms up and open, with arms raised up to the side, means "What's going on here?"

Brushing the palms together means "I'm finished with you" or "I want nothing more to do with it."

Touching the right hand to the heart while shaking hands shows respect.

Twisting a hand upward means "I don't understand."

Moving the head quickly upward means "No."

Moving the head down to one side means "Yes."

In middle school, Syrian boys attend their own schools.

Students who want to continue their education beyond age twelve go on to middle school. At this point, boys and girls attend separate schools. The number of girls in school drops considerably in middle school, especially in the countryside. Only 64 percent of women in Syria can read and write—well below the rate for men, which is 89.7 percent. At the high school level, Syrian students can receive vocational training or prepare for college. An equal number of men and women go to college. Syria's four universities are in Damascus, Aleppo, Latakia, and Homs.

A student reads French at Damascus University.

One Major Religion

Muhammad was the founder of Islam.

S YRIA DOES NOT HAVE AN OFFICIAL RELIGION, AND FREE-dom of religion is guaranteed by Syria's constitution. Islam, however, influences all areas of Syrian life. In fact, the constitution states that Syria's president must be a follower of Islam. It also states that Islamic law is the main source of Syria's laws and government policies. About 90 percent of Syrians are Muslim.

Islamic Beliefs

The prophet Muhammad (570–632) founded Islam in 610 in the city of Mecca in what is now Saudi Arabia. He is said to have received messages from Allah (God) instructing him to preach about Allah's power and goodness. These messages

Opposite: **The shrine of Sayyeda near Damascus**

One Major Religion **89**

A devout Muslim reads the Quran, the holy book of Islam.

were written in the Quran, the Muslims' holy book. Allah is the same God that Christians and Jews worship. Muhammad accepted the Old Testament of the Jews and the New Testament of the Christians as true, but he did not accept Jesus Christ as the son of God. Instead, he believed that Jesus was a great prophet. Muhammad believed that it was his duty to spread Islam throughout the world. After Muhammad's death, his followers brought Islam to Syria when they conquered the area.

The words of Allah in the Quran provide instruction for Muslims in all areas of daily life. The Quran discusses the importance of the family, the roles of women and children, how foods should be prepared, what foods should not be eaten, the importance of cleanliness and modesty in dress, and that living things should not be portrayed in art. Muslims believe that the Quran is God's last word to man.

The Five Pillars of Islam are the Quran's most important rules. The first pillar is *shahadah*, the profession of faith. Muslims must say the words, "There is no God but Allah, and Muhammad is his messenger." The second pillar, *salat*, requires prayer five times a day—at sunrise, midmorning, mid-afternoon, sunset, and nightfall. In villages, a man called a *muezzin* gives the call to prayer from a minaret, a tall, slender tower on a mosque. In the cities, the call is broadcast over loudspeakers. The five daily prayers can take place in a mosque, at home, or outdoors. During prayer, Muslims kneel and bow down facing Mecca, Muhammad's birthplace. Each prayer lasts a few minutes.

Religious Followers in Syria

Sunni Muslims	74%
Alawi Muslims	12%
Christians	10%
Druze Muslims	3%
Other Muslim sects	1%

The Muslim call to prayer is often made from a minaret.

The third pillar, *zakat*, is to give gifts of charity to the poor. *Sawm*, which means fasting, is the fourth pillar. Fasting takes place during the entire month of Ramadan, the ninth month in the Islamic year. During each day of Ramadan, Muslims do not eat or drink between sunrise and sunset. In the evenings, after dark, they have a large meal with their families. The last pillar of Islam is the *hajj*, the pilgrimage to Mecca. If financially possible, all Muslims are expected to make this trip once in their lives. The hajj takes place two months after Ramadan.

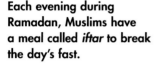

Each evening during Ramadan, Muslims have a meal called *iftar* to break the day's fast.

Friday is the Islamic Sabbath. Thursday night is the beginning of the weekend in Syria. About noon on Fridays, Syria's Muslims gather for prayer in the mosques. Women and men pray separately. Someone reads from the Quran, and an *imam*, a spiritual adviser, gives a sermon. Islam has no priests, ministers, or bishops.

On Fridays, many Muslims, including President Bashar al-Asad (center), go to mosques to pray.

Sufism

Sufism is not another sect of Islam. Instead, it is a mystical part of both the Sunni and Shia sects. Sufis try to detach themselves from the world and its distractions. They do this through prayer and fasting. In groups, Sufis chant, jump, and sway back and forth until they lose touch with the material world and feel God in every part of their body. Other Sufis become whirling dervishes (above). They believe that by spinning in a circle until they cannot feel anything, they become united with God.

The Many Sects of Muslim

After Muhammad's death, Muhammad's followers in Mecca disagreed on whom should be the new leader, called the caliph. Islam split into two branches, Sunni and Shia. The Shia backed Muhammad's son-in-law Ali. They believed that only descendants of Muhammad should be the caliph. The Sunnis backed someone else. Between 656 and 661, this dispute spilled into Syria. When Ali became the caliph, the governor of Syria rebelled. Ali was assassinated, and the Sunni governor became the caliph. Today, Sunni Muslims make up Syria's largest religious group. The Shia make up only a tiny minority.

The other main Muslim sects in Syria—Alawites and Druze—are offshoots of Shia. The Alawites are Syria's largest religious minority. Unlike the Sunni and Shia, the Alawites consider Muhammad divine. They also follow some Christian practices and celebrate some Christian holidays. In Syria, the Alawites live mainly in the Latakia region and in Damascus. Many Alawites have gained positions of power in the government. Hafiz al-Asad was an Alawite. The Druze also have mixed beliefs, including a belief in reincarnation. The Druze don't pray in mosques, Thursday is their Sabbath, and they regard one of their founders as divine. Today, the Druze live mainly in the Hauran area of southern Syria.

Muslim Holidays

Syria's Muslims celebrate a variety of holidays throughout the year. Muharram is the first month of the Islamic calendar. It is a time when Shia mourn the tragic deaths of Muhammad's grandson, Hussein, and his wife and children. This occurred during early warfare between the Sunni and the Shia.

One of the largest Islamic feasts is Eid al-Fitr, which means "the breaking of the fast." This great feast comes at the end of Ramadan, the month of fasting. Eid al-Fitr lasts for three days.

Syrians celebrate this feast with special foods, such as desserts filled with dates, pistachios, pine nuts, and almonds. Many Syrians also buy new clothes at this time. Then they visit family and friends. Syrian children sometimes receive money from their relatives. Fireworks and carnival rides are also part of the fun of Eid al-Fitr.

Eid al-Adha, the feast of the lamb, marks the end of the hajj, the pilgrimage to Mecca. This feast, which also lasts three days, is in remembrance of Abraham's obedience to God's command to kill his son, Ishmael. Seeing Abraham's obedience, God had Abraham kill a lamb instead. Today, Muslims have a cow, goat, or sheep slaughtered. They give one-third of the meat to the poor and another third to relatives. They prepare the last third for the family feast.

Christians and Jews

Before Islam came to Syria, most Syrians were Christians and Jews. The Jewish community had roots in Syria going back thousands of years. By the time Syria became independent in 1946, about 30,000 Jews were living there. But tensions created by the Arab-Israeli conflict made life miserable for Syria's Jews. Thousands left in the 1950s. Those who stayed faced harsh discrimination. In 1992, President Hafiz al-Asad allowed most of Syria's remaining Jews to leave the country. Today, there are only a few hundred Jews left in Syria.

The Umayyad Mosque

Every Syrian village, town, and city has a mosque. Each mosque is positioned so that during prayer, the faithful are facing Mecca. Syria's most famous mosque is the Umayyad Mosque in Damascus.

The site of the Umayyad Mosque has seen much of Syria's religious history. First, the Aramaeans built a temple there to Haddad, one of their gods. Then the Romans constructed a temple to their god Jupiter. Finally, the Christians built a church dedicated to John the Baptist. During the early 700s, an Umayyad caliph tore down the church and had the mosque built. It took ten years.

Over the years, the mosque has been rebuilt three times because of invasions, fire, and an earthquake. The mosque's three minarets, however, have survived since the 700s. The Umayyad Mosque is believed to have the first minarets built anywhere in the Islamic world. Outside the mosque's courtyard is a garden with the tomb of the great military leader Salah ad-Din. Inside the mosque is a shrine to John the Baptist.

A large number of Christians still live in Syria. Most probably have roots going back to some of the world's first Christians. The Apostle Paul is the most famous early Christian with links to Syria. He was a Jew who persecuted early Christians. Then one day on the road to Damascus, he had a vision that caused him to became a follower of Christ. He spread Christianity to what today are Turkey, Greece, and Italy. Most Syrian Christians belong to Catholic or Eastern Orthodox churches.

Throughout Syria, there are many famous Catholic and Orthodox churches. One of the oldest is the Church of Saint George in Ezra, which dates to 515. Saint George died defending Christianity against the Roman emperor Diocletian. It is now a Greek Orthodox church. North of Damascus, the Syrian Catholic church and monastery of Marmoosa look out over the desert. Today the monastery, which dates back to the 1000s, provides food and lodging to travelers. In exchange, guests are expected to help make meals or do other chores.

The Christian holiday of Christmas is celebrated in a more subdued manner in Syria than in the United States. On Christmas Eve, families build a fire in the yard and sing hymns. On Christmas Day, Christian families attend mass. Rather than Santa Claus, Syrian children look for the little camel who leaves gifts on Epiphany, the twelfth day after Christmas. This harkens back to the story of the three wise men who brought gifts to the baby Jesus.

Opposite: **Many Christians in Syria belong to the Greek Orthodox church.**

Rich Cultural Traditions

SYRIA'S LONG HISTORY HAS GIVEN RISE TO A RICH CULTURAL heritage. Its traditional culture ranges from classical Arab poetry to intricate metalwork. Syrians still enjoy these arts. Many Syrian writers, artists, musicians, and filmmakers have also made contributions to modern culture.

Opposite: **A Syrian dancer**

Syria's writers and artists do not have full freedom of expression. They are not allowed to criticize the government. Restrictions on their freedom have caused many talented writers and artists to leave Syria. In addition, the government censors books, magazines, and newspapers that come into Syria from other countries.

Books and newspapers in Syria are censored.

Throughout the centuries, Syrian craftspeople have worked with cloth, wood, and metal to create beautiful objects for everyday use. Islamic rules forbid portraying people or animals in artwork. For that reason, craftspeople use geometric patterns, flowers, fruits, and calligraphy as designs in their work.

Syrian fabric is known throughout the world. In fact, the fabric called damask is named for the city of Damascus, where the first damask was made. Damask is a heavy silk or cotton fabric with intricate geometric or floral designs. Tablecloths and cushion covers are often made of damask. Another fabric first made in Syria is brocade. Brocade is a silk fabric with

Damask cloth gets its name from the city of Damascus.

Syria has long been famous for its marquetry.

raised patterns of gold and silver thread. Syrians are also famous for making hand-knotted rugs with sheep's or goat's wool. These carpets are called *kilims*. Some Syrian carpets are still handmade, mainly by Bedouin women, although most carpets are now machine-made in factories.

Syria has a strong woodworking tradition as well. The country is especially famous for its marquetry, the process of inlaying mother-of-pearl or polished bone in wood. Jewelry boxes, coffee tables, chests, chessboards, and stands to hold the Quran are usually decorated in this way. Sometimes entire wall panels are made with inlays. Antique Syrian marquetry is delicately beautiful. Today, however, plastic is often used for the inlays.

Ornate metalwork

Metalworking is another important Syrian craft. At one time, Syria was known for Damascus steel, which was used to make knives and sword blades. Damascus steel is an extremely hard steel with a wavy pattern. Another Syrian metal process is called damascening. In this process, silver or gold is inlayed into other metals, such as steel, copper, or brass. Trays, tea sets, and candlesticks were often made in this way. Today, precious metals are seldom used for damascening.

Glassblowing is another traditional Syrian craft. Vases, glasses, bottles, and large water pipes called *nargilehs* were once all made from blown glass.

Unfortunately, the quality of traditional Syrian crafts is declining. Younger people are not as interested in learning the crafts, so the skills are not being handed down to the next generation. To counter this trend, the Syrian government has started programs to teach these skills.

In cafés and restaurants, Syrians enjoy listening to musicians who play traditional Arab instruments. Syrians also buy recordings of both traditional and popular songs.

The most famous Arab musical instrument is the *oud*, a large stringed instrument that looks something like a lute. Another stringed instrument is the *qanun*. The qanun is laid horizontally when it is played. Its strings are plucked rather than strummed. The *rababa* has one string that makes a wailing sound. A high-pitched sound comes from the *nay*, a kind of flute. Common percussion instruments in Syrian music include tambourines, *daffs* (sets of cymbals), and drums. The *tabla* is a flat drum that rests on the player's lap. The *dirbakka* is a larger drum that stands on the floor.

An oud salesman at a market in Aleppo

Syrians enjoy many styles of singing. Farid al-Atrache's blend of Arabic and Western music became popular in the 1940s. Cassettes of his songs remain big sellers in Syria. On the other hand, Sabah Fakhri is known as the master of traditional Arab songs. Born in 1933 in Aleppo, Fakhri has made hundreds of records and once sang for ten hours straight. This earned him a place in the *Guinness Book of Records*. Younger performers include George Wassouf, who sings Syrian folk songs. He is considered Syria's biggest star. Nur Mahaha is the king of Syrian popular music.

George Wassouf began his career at age twelve, singing at parties in his hometown of Homs.

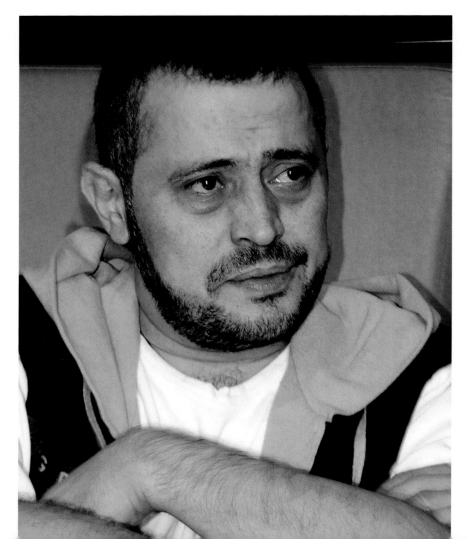

Dancing is also part of Syria's culture. The *debke* is a popular folk dance. It is mainly performed at weddings and other celebrations. In this high-spirited dance, people hold hands to form a circle and then move to the music. Other dances are only performed by experts. For instance, the sword dance is only performed by skilled swordsmen.

Syrians have been making films since the 1928 silent film *Under the Sky of Damascus*. In the 1960s, Dureid Lahham and Nihad al-Qali starred in several successful comedies. In the 1980s and 1990s, most films dealt with social issues with a historical background. The 1981 film *The Half-Meter Incident* shows the effect of the Six-Day War on an office worker.

Folk dancers perform for an audience in Aleppo.

Mohammed Malas's 1984 film *Dreams of the City* is set during the political upheavals of the 1950s. Nabil al-Maleh's 1993 film *The Extras* presents a sad love story while criticizing some Muslim customs.

Literature

Syria's literary history goes back more than a thousand years. In the 900s, writers in Syria were part of the golden age of Arab literature. These early poets used formal, flowery language. Abu al-Tayyib al-Mutanabbi (915–965) was one of the greatest Arab poets. From 949 to 957, he served as the court poet of Aleppo's ruler. Although al-Mutanabbi wrote long poems in praise of military victories, his poems are best-known for expressing his moods.

Abu al-Ala al-Maarri (973–1058) is considered the best of the classical writers. Al-Maarri's poems had deep philosophical and religious themes. In prose writings, he used animal characters to comment on political events. His best-known prose work is *The Epistle of Forgiveness*, which is set in Heaven and in Hell.

After this era of poets, Syrian literature went into decline for several centuries. Then during the 1900s, more writers picked up their pens. Many of them criticized the government and had to leave Syria. One of Syria's leading poets was Nizar Qabbani (1923–1998). Qabbani used everyday language in his poems, which criticized Arab culture and the humiliation of defeat in the Six-Day War. The government forced him to leave the country. When Qabbani died, President Hafiz al-Asad had his body brought back to Damascus to be buried. A street was also named after him. Another leading poet, Ali Ahmad Said (1930–), left Syria and now lives in Paris, France. He writes under the name Adonis. He believes poems should appeal to the mind and not the emotions. He also sees poems as political weapons.

Syria also has important fiction writers. Ghada al-Sammam (1940–) is Syria's best-known woman writer. In a collection of short stories called *Your Eyes Are My Destiny*, al-Sammam looks at the life of women in a world controlled by men. Walid Ikhlassy writes novels and plays while also serving in Syria's Parliament. In *Al-Futuhat*, he portrays an imaginary country torn apart by authoritarian government. Although the Syrian government censors literature, the book was published. It received harsh reviews, however.

Ali Ahmad Said has written more than thirty books.

Art and Architecture

In ancient Syria, art and architecture went hand in hand. At Palmyra, for example, relief sculptures were carved into the stone pillars and arches. These reliefs were usually of gods, rulers, and animals. Later, Islamic law forbade the use of human or animal figures. In mosques, palaces, and citadels, artists made geometric designs using mosaics. Throughout Syria, examples of Roman, Byzantine, Arab, and Ottoman architecture can still be seen. Although the architecture at Palmyra and the amphitheater at Bosra are ruins, other important buildings such as Crac des Chevaliers and the Umayyad Mosque still stand.

The idea of art that is not intended to decorate a building is fairly new in Syria. One of Syria's earliest painters was

Carvings at the Roman Temple of Bel in Palmyra were made nearly two thousand years ago.

UNESCO World Cultural Heritage Sites

The United Nations Educational, Scientific, and Cultural Organization (UNESCO) identifies sites around the world that are vital to the world's cultural heritage. Once a site is on the World Cultural Heritage list, it is protected from being torn down or changed.

Syria has four sites on the list. Syria's sites are entire sections of cities and an entire ruin site rather than just being one building or one statue. They are the Ancient City of Damascus, the Ancient City of Bosra, the Ancient City of Aleppo, and the ruins of Palmyra.

Tawfeek Tarek (1875–1940). He painted scenes from historical events, as well as portraits and landscapes. Mahmoud Jalal (1911–1975) portrayed working people as heroes. Other modern artists have used traditional geometric designs and calligraphy in an abstract style. Mahmoud Hammad (1923–1988) founded the Arabic letterism movement, a group of artists whose art was based on calligraphy. Syria's best-known artist today is Fateh Moudarres (1922–). He uses dark colors and gives his people sad, child-like expressions. Zouhair Dabbagh is Syria's leading sculptor. From his studio in

Mosaic decoration in the Great Mosque

Aleppo, he creates pieces that reflect the human misery caused by wars. The works of many of these artists are in the National Museum in Damascus.

The National Museum

A visit to the National Museum in Damascus provides a good overview of Syria's history and culture. Visitors enter the museum through the gateway taken from a palace west of Palmyra. The palace was built in 688, and the gateway was brought stone by stone to Damascus and rebuilt. One of the museum's most important exhibits displays the stone tablets from Ugarit with the world's first alphabet. The wall of another room is covered in marquetry. A Jewish synagogue from the 100s was also reconstructed on the museum's grounds.

Syria's Olympic Stars

Syria won its first, and so far only, gold medal during the 1996 Olympic Games in Atlanta, Georgia. The Syrian who brought this honor to her country was Ghada Shouaa. Born in Mahrda in 1972, Shouaa began her athletic career on the basketball court. She played on Syria's national team for a few years. Then she turned to the heptathlon. This sport is made up of seven track-and-field events: the 200- and 800-meter dashes, the 100-meter hurdles, the high jump, the long jump, the shot put, and the javelin throw. In 1991, Shouaa competed in her first heptathlon. Although she placed last, she continued practicing and training. In 1995, she placed first in the World Championship Games. Then in 1996, she won the Olympic gold. In

2000, Shouaa attempted to defend her Olympic title, but injuries forced her to drop out of the competition. Since then, she has not been involved in sports.

Syria has two other Olympic medalists. In 1984, Joe Atiyeh won a silver medal in wrestling at the Los Angeles Olympics. At the 2004 Olympics in Athens, Al Shami Naser won a bronze medal in boxing.

Sports

As in many Middle Eastern countries, soccer is the most popular sport in Syria. Children play the game whenever they get the chance. Syria also has several professional teams and a national team that competes in international games. Basketball is another popular sport in Syria.

Since Bashar al-Asad became president, he has emphasized individual fitness. Several large public sports complexes are available in Damascus, Aleppo, and Latakia. Syrians may use the complexes' swimming pools, tennis courts, and running tracks free of charge. Large hotels offer memberships to the public for use of their pools, courts, and fitness equipment.

Family, Fun, and Food

SPENDING TIME WITH FAMILY AND FRIENDS IS AT THE HEART of Syrian life. Syrians like nothing better than to while away the hours talking with those close to them. Syrians are also renowned for their hospitality. They will often invite someone they've just met to join them for dinner at home. Syrians are equally generous and welcoming to visitors from other countries.

Opposite: **A Syrian girl in traditional dress**

Syrian Food

Delicious foods are the highlight of many social gatherings in Syria. Syrian food is known for being either very sweet or very sour. For example, the Pepsi and 7-Up that are bottled in Syria are much sweeter than the same beverages bottled in the rest

Syrians serve their strong coffee in small cups.

Kebabs are a popular food in Syria.

of the world. Much of Syria's sugar crop goes into these sweet drinks as well as into their desserts. The sour flavor of yogurt and Syrian pickles is also popular. Other seasonings commonly used by Syrian cooks include mint, parsley, garlic, and lemon. For the most part, Syrians do not use knives, forks, or spoons. Instead, they either pick the food up directly or scoop it up with a piece of bread or meat.

Most Syrians eat three meals a day. Breakfast takes place very early in the morning, after the first call to prayer. A Syrian breakfast might include toasted pita bread, yogurt dip, *halabi* (string cheese), olives, and sliced cucumber. Other choices are breakfast cookies, bread and apricot jelly, and melons. Strong, thick, sweet *ahwa* (coffee) and tea are the main beverages.

Lunch is served in the afternoon. For lunch, Syrians might have *tabouleh*, a salad made of tomatoes, onions, parsley, bulgur wheat, dried mint, and lemon juice. People scoop up this salad with pieces of lettuce. Pita bread stuffed with fried vegetables is another lunch choice. A soup made with warm yogurt, rice, and small meatballs is common in the winter.

Dinner is served late in Syria's cities, starting between 8 and 10 P.M. Popular dishes include shish kebabs with lamb, onions, and other vegetables grilled on a skewer; *yebrat*, meat-stuffed grape leaves; or chicken and olives on rice.

Menu for a Syrian Party

Food at a Syrian party is a treat for the eyes, nose, and mouth. The following items might be found on a typical Syrian party table:

Appetizers
Triangle-shaped phyllo dough stuffed with spinach and cheese
Triangle-shaped phyllo dough stuffed with ground meat or vegetables
Grape leaves stuffed with vegetables or meat
Hummus and pita bread for dipping

Main dishes
Rice with meat, tomatoes, and raisins
Creamed spinach
Meat-filled pie

Desserts
Lemon-orange cookies
Layered phyllo dough with pistachios and rose-water syrup

Hummus: A National Dish

Hummus is a thick mixture of mashed chickpeas and sesame paste. It is used as a dip or spread inside pita bread. Syrians serve hummus at most meals.

Ingredients:

1 can of chickpeas

1 clove of minced garlic

2 tablespoons of sesame seed paste (tahini)

$\frac{1}{2}$ cup of lemon juice

Pinch of salt

1. Save half the liquid from the can of chickpeas. Then place this liquid, the chickpeas, garlic, and sesame seed paste in a blender.

2. Add the lemon juice and salt.

3. Blend until smooth. If the mixture is too thick, add a little more lemon juice, until it's ready for dipping. Pita bread is cut into wedges and dipped in the hummus. Cooked meat or raw vegetables can also be dipped.

Syrians love to snack. Between meals, they might stop at a food stand and pick up sandwiches. *Shwarma* is pita bread stuffed with lamb or chicken. A *falafel* sandwich is made of flattened balls of ground chickpeas, along with lettuce and tomato. *Mezze*, or appetizers, also make good snacks. They include *hummus*, a dip of ground chickpeas and sesame paste, and *baba ghanoug*, a smoky, smashed eggplant dip. Other appetizers are made by stuffing phyllo dough and grape leaves with meat or vegetable mixtures.

Syrians love sweets, so their desserts are rich, sweet, and sticky. *Mahalabiye* is a milk custard with orange flavoring, almonds, and pistachios. *Baklawa* is made with layers of phyllo dough, crushed pistachios or almonds, and orange or rose-water syrup. *Barazi* is a large cookie with pistachios and sesame seeds.

Different Kinds of Homes

Housing in Syria varies from the city to rural areas. Most people in Syria's cities live in apartments. Some Syrians own their apartments, while others rent. An average apartment has a kitchen, a bathroom, a bedroom, and a multipurpose living room. The living room also serves as the dining area and perhaps as a place for someone to sleep. Water for the kitchen and bathroom is sometimes stored in a rooftop tank. Electricity is not available all the time, and electrical service is marked by timed outages. Syrians time their use of electrical appliances around these outages. Rural housing is mainly

An apartment building in Aleppo

single-family homes. Each home is built around its own courtyard. Most villages have running water and electricity.

High ceilings make homes cooler in the hot summers. Few homes have air-conditioning, so Syrians rely on fans. The floors and sometimes the walls of Syrian homes are covered by kilims. Most Syrian homes have couches and chairs, but many people also provide cushions and pillows for seating. Large chandeliers hang from the high ceilings of Syrian homes.

In parts of northern Syria, some people have houses that look like beehives. These homes are made of straw and mud, and stay cool in the summer and warm in the winter. Kilims and pillows cover the floors.

In northern Syria, some people live in beehive-shaped homes.

Syrian Clothing

Many Syrians wear a combination of Western-style and traditional clothing. They all dress modestly, however. Neither men nor women wear shorts or sleeveless shirts. Women's skirts and dresses cover the knee or touch the ground. Some women wear head scarves. Some men wear long gowns called *jalabiyyehs*, along with cotton head cloths called *kafeeyehs* that are held in place by an *aqal*, a black cord. The headgear and long gowns protect Syrians from the sand and heat. Bedouins and some Kurds wear their own colorful traditional clothing.

Syrian Weddings

Traditionally in Syria, marriages were arranged by parents or other family members. Today, young people have more freedom to choose whom they marry, but they still must win their parents' approval.

In Syria, the groom's family pays for the wedding. Weddings can go on for several days and be quite expensive. Food must be provided for the many guests, and musicians are hired for entertainment and dancing. If the wedding is held in a home, the groom, his male relatives and friends, and the bride's male relatives first have a party outside among themselves. Meanwhile, inside the house, the bride, her female relatives and friends, and the groom's female relatives eat and talk and dance with one another. When the women are through eating, the men come in and eat. Then the men and women dance together. Wealthy people usually hold the wedding in a hotel or large restaurant. At some point during the festivities, the marriage contract is signed.

Many couples choose to have a white wedding. The groom wears a suit and the bride a Western-style wedding gown. More traditional clothing is worn at weddings in villages. The bride's dress might be red or black, with colorful embroidery. She also wears an elaborate headdress. The groom dresses in a long gown and wears the traditional male head cloth.

National Holidays in Syria

New Year's Day	January 1
Orthodox Christmas	January 7
Revolution Day	March 8
Easter	Sunday in March or April
Evacuation Day	April 17
May Day	May 1
Martyr's Day	May 6
Christmas	December 25

The following Muslim holidays are also public holidays. Their dates vary from year to year:

Islamic New Year's Day

Muhammad's Birthday

Eid al-Fitr

Eid al-Adha

Holidays

Many of Syria's holidays are religious, but a few are not. Martyr's Day is celebrated on May 6. It marks the execution of twenty-one men who worked to overthrow the Ottoman Turks in 1915. Syrians place wreaths in public places to honor those men.

Revolution Day is celebrated on March 8. This holiday marks the revolution in Syria's government that took place in March 1963 when the Baath Party gained power. The main events of Revolution Day are big rallies where government leaders give speeches.

On April 17, Evacuation Day is observed. On that day in 1946, the last French soldiers left Syria, and the Syrian Arab

Syrian women attend a conference on literacy in Homs.

Republic became an independent country. To prepare for Evacuation Day, children make flags at school to use at home. Then, on April 17, Syrian flags fly proudly from homes and along streets.

Separate Lives

Women and men lead separate lives in Syria. Women take care of the home and raise the children. They socialize at home with other women, mainly other female family members. When girls are not in school, they are expected to stay close to home. As more women attend universities and have careers outside the home, they are coming into more contact with men. But while Syrian laws give women equality, Islamic traditions control their activities within the family.

Most Syrian men remain in their parents' home until they marry. But boys and men are free to come and go as they please. A favorite male pastime is going to a coffeehouse or café. There they drink coffee and tea, talk, play cards and trictrac (backgammon), and smoke the narghile. The narghile, also called the hubble-bubble, is a large water pipe through which tobacco is smoked.

Men enjoy a game of backgammon in Aleppo.

Going to the *hammam*, or bathhouse, is another popular male activity. There men might take a bath, sit in a sauna, have a rubdown with a horsehair glove, or have a vigorous massage. A few hammams are strictly for women, while other hammams set aside a few hours a week just for women.

Aleppo's Hammam al-Nasri is probably the grandest bathhouse in Syria.

Vendors sell lace at a souq in Damascus.

Both men and women shop in the souqs, large market-places in the cities. Each merchant in the souq has a separate stall or booth. Souqs are organized by type of goods. Textiles are in one area, foods in another, jewelry in another, and so on. Souqs are a feast for the senses. They are filled with brightly colored cloth, the intense aroma of spices, and the banter between buyers and sellers. They are bustling, vibrant places. In their crowded and narrow aisles, the past meets the present in Syria.

Timeline

Syrian History		World History	
	About		
People first live in Syria.	**148,000** B.C.		
Damascus and Aleppo are founded.	**3000** B.C.		
Amorites, Hittites, Egyptians, Hebrews, Canaanites, Aramaeans, and others move into Syria.	**2200–1200** B.C.	**2500** B.C.	Egyptians build the Pyramids and the Sphinx in Giza.
Syria becomes part of the Persian Empire.	**539** B.C.	**563** B.C.	The Buddha is born in India.
Alexander the Great conquers Syria.	**332** B.C.		
Syria comes under Roman rule.	**64** B.C.	A.D. **313**	The Roman emperor Constantine recognizes Christianity.
Arab Muslims take control of Syria.	A.D. **635**	**610**	The Prophet Muhammad begins preaching a new religion called Islam.
Damascus becomes the capital of the Umayyad caliphate.	**661**	**1054**	The Eastern (Orthodox) and Western (Roman) Churches break apart.
		1066	William the Conqueror defeats the English in the Battle of Hastings.
European Christian Crusaders invade Syria.	**1098**	**1095**	Pope Urban II proclaims the First Crusade.
The Mamelukes gain control of Syria.	**1250**	**1215**	King John seals the Magna Carta.
		1300s	The Renaissance begins in Italy.
		1347	The Black Death sweeps through Europe.
		1453	Ottoman Turks capture Constantinople, conquering the Byzantine Empire.
		1492	Columbus arrives in North America.
The Ottoman Turks take control of Syria.	**1516**	**1500s**	The Reformation leads to the birth of Protestantism.
		1776	The Declaration of Independence is signed.
		1789	The French Revolution begins.
		1865	The American Civil War ends.

Syrian History

France is given control over Syria.	1920
Syria becomes independent.	1946
Syria fights a war against Israel.	1948–1949
Syria joins Egypt to form the United Arab Republic (UAR).	1958
Syria withdraws from the UAR.	1961
The Baath Party takes over Syria's government.	1963
During the Six-Day War with Israel, Syria loses the Golan Heights.	1967
Hafiz al-Asad takes control of Syria in a military coup.	1970
Hafiz al-Asad becomes Syria's president.	1971
Syria and Egypt attack Israel.	1975
Syria intervenes in the Lebanese civil war.	1976
An uprising led by the Muslim Brotherhood in Hama is brutally put down.	1982
Syria sends troops to Saudi Arabia to assist in the Gulf War against Iraq.	1990
Many Jews leave Syria.	1992
Hafiz al-Asad dies; Bashar al-Assad becomes president, releases political prisoners, and legalizes private banks.	2000
Assad legalizes private schools and universities and allows an independent newspaper to be published.	2001
Syria signs trade agreements with the European Union and withdraws all troops from Lebanon.	2005

World History

1914	World War I breaks out.
1917	The Bolshevik Revolution brings communism to Russia.
1929	Worldwide economic depression begins.
1939	World War II begins, following the German invasion of Poland.
1945	World War II ends.
1957	The Vietnam War starts.
1969	Humans land on the moon.
1975	The Vietnam War ends.
1979	Soviet Union invades Afghanistan.
1983	Drought and famine in Africa.
1989	The Berlin Wall is torn down, as communism crumbles in Eastern Europe.
1991	Soviet Union breaks into separate states.
1992	Bill Clinton is elected U.S. president.
2000	George W. Bush is elected U.S. president.
2001	Terrorists attack World Trade Towers, New York and the Pentagon, Washington, D.C.

Fast Facts

Official name: Syrian Arab Republic

Capital: Damascus

Official language: Arabic

Damascus

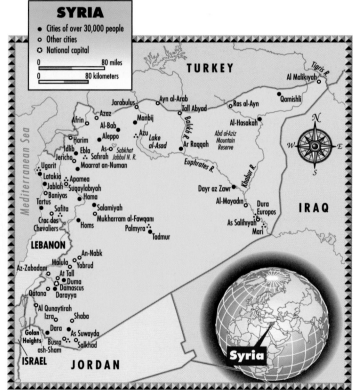

Syria's flag

Orchards

Year of founding:	1946
National anthem:	"An-Nashid as-Suri" ("Defenders of the Realm")
Government:	Socialist republic under authoritarian regime
Chief of state:	President
Area:	71,504 square miles (185,170 sq km)
Length east to west:	515 miles (829 km)
Length north to south:	465 miles (748 km)
Borders:	Turkey to the north; Iraq to the east and south; Jordan to the south; Israel, Lebanon, and the Mediterranean Sea to the west
Highest elevation:	Mount Hermon in Israeli-occupied Golan Heights, 9,232 feet (2,814 m)
Lowest elevation:	Near Lake Tiberias, 656 feet (200 m) below sea level
Average temperature extremes:	In January, 41°F (5°C); in July, 104°F (40°C)
Average precipitation extremes:	40 inches (127 cm) along the coast; less than 5 inches (13 cm) in the southeastern desert
National population (2004 estimate):	19,230,000

Umayyad Mosque

Syrian currency

Population of largest cities (2004 estimate):

Aleppo	2,000,000
Damascus	1,700,000
Homs	715,500
Latakia	303,000
Hama	273,000

Famous landmarks:
- ▶ *Azem Palace*, Damascus
- ▶ *Dead Cities*, north of Aleppo
- ▶ *Ruins at Palmyra*
- ▶ *Roman Amphitheatre*, Bosra
- ▶ *Umayyad Mosque*, Damascus

Industry: Trade, tourism, and government services make up the largest part of Syria's economy. Refining oil and making cotton cloth and other textiles are the leading industries. Other important products include beverages, cement, fertilizer, and processed foods. Syria's most important mineral products are oil and phosphate.

Currency: The unit of currency is the Syrian pound (SYP). In March 2005, one U.S. dollar equaled 51.9 Syrian pounds.

Weights and measures: Metric system

Literacy rate: 76.9 percent

Folk dancers

Ghada Shouaa

Common Arabic words and phrases:

addaysh essa'aa?	What time is it?
'afwan	You're welcome.
ahwa	Coffee
aiwa	Yes
bi addaysh?	How much is it?
chai	Tea
khoobz	Bread
kayf Haalak?	How are you?
keef boosal ala . . .?	How do I get to . . .?
la	No
ma'a salaama	Good-bye
marHaba	Hi
min fadlak	Please
shu-ismak?	What is your name?
shukran	Thank-you
wayn . . ?	Where is . . .?

Famous people:

Bashar al-Asad (1965–)
President of Syria

Hafiz al-Asad (1930–2000)
President of Syria (1971–2000)

Sabah Fakhiri (1933–)
Singer of traditional music

Fateh Moudarres (1922–)
Artist

Ali Ahmad Said (1930–)
Poet and literary critic

Salah ad-Din (1137–1193)
Great military leader

Ghada al-Sammam (1940–)
Writer

Ghada Shouaa (1972–)
Olympic track and field athlete

Sa'dallah Wannus (1941–)
Playwright

To Find Out More

Nonfiction

▶ Morrison, John. *Syria*. Creation of the Modern Middle East series. Philadelphia: Chelsea House Publishers, 2003.

▶ Skinner, Patricia. *Syria*. Milwaukee, Wis.: Gareth Stevens Publishing, 2005.

▶ Sullivan, Anne Marie. *Syria*. Philadelphia: Mason Crest Publishers, 2004.

Recordings

▶ *The Aleppian Music Room: The Art of Classical Arab Singing.* Le Chant du Monde label, 1998. *Music of famous classical Syrian singers and musicians.*

▶ *The Whirling Dervishes of Damascus.* Le Chant du Monde label, 1999. *The music of Sufi singers in a whirling dervish ritual.*

Web Sites

▶ **Golan**
www.golan-syria.org
Reports on the geography, history, and politics of the Golan Heights from Syria's point of view.

▶ **Ministry of Tourism**
www.syriatourism.org
For tourist information as well as material on the history and culture of Syria.

▶ **Syrian Arab News Agency**
www.sana.org
For daily news stories, reports, and press releases on the economy, politics, culture, and tourism of Syria.

Embassies

▶ **Embassy of the Syrian Arab Republic**
2215 Wyoming Avenue, NW
Washington, DC 20008
(202) 232-6313

Index

Page numbers in *italics* indicate illustrations.

Meet the Author

Patricia K. Kummer writes and edits textbook materials and nonfiction books for children and young adults from her home office in Lisle, Illinois. She earned a bachelor of arts in history from the College of Saint Catherine in Saint Paul, Minnesota, and a master's degree in history from Marquette University in Milwaukee, Wisconsin. Before starting her career in publishing, she taught social studies in junior high school.

Kummer has written biographies, books about the states, and books about American, African, Asian, and European history. Her books include *Cameroon*, *Côte d'Ivoire*, *Korea*, *Singapore*, *Tibet*, and *Ukraine* in the Children's Press series Enchantment of the World. She also wrote *Currency* and *The Calendar* in the Franklin Watts series Inventions That Shaped the World. In addition to writing, Kummer teaches adults at the College of Du Page how to write nonfiction books for children and serves as an elected trustee on the Lisle Library Board.

"Writing books about people, states, and countries requires a great deal of research," Kummer says. "My method of research began by going online. There, I compiled a list of the most recent books on Syria. Many of the books were at my public library. For the books my library did not have, I placed interlibrary loan requests. To keep up with events in Syria, I received updates from Internet news sites. I also found several other Web sites with solid information on Syria."

Photo Credits